The Mirror Mind

William Johnston

THE MIRROR MIND

Spirituality and Transformation

Published in San Francisco by
HARPER & ROW PUBLISHERS
Cambridge, Hagerstown, Philadelphia, New York
London, Mexico City, São Paulo, Sydney

THE MIRROR MIND: *Spirituality and Transformation*. Copyright © 1981 by William Johnston. All rights reserved. Printed in the United States of America. No part of this book may be used or reproduced in any manner whatsoever without written permission except in the case of brief quotations embodied in critical articles and reviews. For information address Harper & Row, Publishers, Inc., 10 East 53rd Street, New York, NY 10022. Published simultaneously in Canada by Fitzhenry & Whiteside, Limited, Toronto.

FIRST EDITION

Designed by Leigh McLellan

Library of Congress Cataloging in Publication Data

Johnston, William, 1925–
   The mirror mind.

   Includes index.
   1. Mysticism—Addresses, essays, lectures.
2. Spiritual life—Addresses, essays, lectures.
3. Christianity and other religions—Buddhism—
Addresses, essays, lectures. 4. Buddhism—Relations—Christianity—Addresses, essays, lectures. I. Title.
   BL625.J625 1981   248.4   80-8350
   ISBN 0-06-064197-5

---

81 82 83 84 85 10 9 8 7 6 5 4 3 2 1

For the English Jesuits

Contents

Preface

T HIS BOOK IS based on eight lectures I was invited to give in Oxford in the fall of 1980 in honor of the late Martin D'Arcy, Master of Campion Hall. Asked to speak about "Christianity in Dialogue with Eastern Mysticism," I selected the eight topics that form the eight chapters of this book. All are concerned with mysticism or mystical theology.

It was not easy to find an overall title for the book, and I ended up with *The Mirror Mind.* Buddhism loves to speak about the mind as a mirror—sometimes an empty mirror, sometimes a mirror that reflects the universe. And Christian mystics also speak of the ground of the soul as a mirror that reflects the glory of God and the beauty of the human person. When Buddhists and Christians look into the mirror that is their own mind and heart they find themselves united in a wonderful way.

The first chapter treats of the Buddhist-Christian dialogue, which future generations will surely regard as a high point in the evolution of the religious consciousness of mankind. Here I outline a practical way of dialogue I hope will be acceptable to Buddhists and Christians alike; it is a way that can lead us not only to increased knowledge but also to enlightenment or conversion. The subsequent chapters treat of a Christian spirituality engaged in dialogue with Buddhism and deepening its mystical life.

I write throughout as a Christian and from a Christian standpoint; nor do I claim to speak authoritatively about Buddhism. I believe with Augustine and Anselm that one cannot really understand a religion unless one believes it. *Crede ut intelligas:* Believe that you may understand. The committed Buddhist alone can speak authoritatively about Buddhism, as the committed Christian alone can speak authoritatively about Christianity. In dialogue with another religion one must always be aware of one's limitations; and I hope that I am aware of mine.

Many people have influenced me in the writing of this book. I wish especially to thank Juan Rivera and Rich Devine with whom I discussed many of the problems and who kindly read my manuscript. Then I am deeply grateful to Lin Huei Mei who typed and edited the manuscript and drew the Chinese characters that appear in the text. Finally, I wish to thank Laureen Grady, Rich Curé and Edward Perez Valera who read the manuscript and made valuable suggestions for improvement.

Sophia University
Tokyo

1

*Interreligious Dialogue**

O VER THE PAST decade, mankind has made remarkable progress in the art of dialogue. After much war and terrorism and violence and misunderstanding, enlightened people everywhere begin to see that we must listen to one another, understand one another, know one another, respect one another, love one another. Otherwise we will perish; for dialogue is no longer a luxury but a condition for survival.

And while dialogue extends itself to all areas of human life and activity, it is particularly relevant in the realm of religion. For it is no secret that religion, which should unite men and women at a deep level, has frequently been divisive and has even led to holy and less holy wars. And so, anxious to remedy this situation and to heal the wounds of the past, Buddhists and Christians (and believers in the other great faiths of the world) are quietly coming together to talk and to meditate, giving witness to a world that longs for peace.

Moreover the scope of this dialogue is widening. Christian scholars

*Because I find it difficult to express the universal dimension of human nature in clear and rhythmical English, I have retained traditional generic language in this book. I ask my readers to understand that by *he* I mean "he or she," by *his* I mean "his or hers" and by *mankind* I mean all people.

are seriously studying Buddhist sutras, while Buddhists comment insightfully on Christian scriptures. High-school students are studying world religions; university students are interested in oriental and occidental meditation; popular books and magazines contain references to the great religions of mankind. Christianity has made an enormous impact on Japanese literature since Meiji, while Buddhism has influenced much literature in the West. And all this means that the most unsuspecting people, confronted with the spectacle of great and powerful religions other than their own, are willy-nilly drawn into an interreligious dialogue.

No one can doubt that this interchange will be of the utmost importance not only for the great religions themselves but for the world at large. It may prove to be one of the most significant happenings in the history of our converging universe. Let me, then, speak about it, frankly facing its difficulties and struggles. I shall speak from my own Christian standpoint, leaving it to Buddhists to speak from the perspective of their own religious commitment.

Theological Background

I

Like most developments in our modern world, religious dialogue has its roots in the past. From the sixteenth century, Christian missionaries have been locked in dialogue with Buddhists in Asia, while more recently Buddhists are dialoguing with Christians in the West. But only now, perhaps, are we reaching a point when it becomes possible to evaluate the great missionary effort that began on April 7, 1541, when Francis Xavier, on his thirty-fifth birthday, set sail from Lisbon for Goa, and subsequently for Malacca and Japan.

But here let me be frank. From our vantage point at the end of the twentieth century, the Christian missions seem to have done a remarkably bad job in the area of dialogue. And in recent times a number of people have said so, loudly and lengthily. Were not the missionaries implacable enemies of non-Christian religions? Did they not destroy the culture of the countries to which they brought the gospel? Were they not imperialists who traveled in the black ships of the colonizers? Were they not religious and cultural conquistadors?

Such accusations, alas, are often heard. Nor would I entirely deny their validity. But let us not judge the missionaries too quickly or too harshly. Let us understand them in context. Children of their time, they were born into and nurtured by a European culture that was incorrigibly chauvinistic, that saw itself as *the* culture, the norm by which other cultures should be judged. People who did not belong to this culture were barbarians to whom one could do no better service than that of lifting them out of their absymal ignorance. A similar way of thinking, it must be admitted, existed in ancient Israel, in Greece, in Rome, in India, in China and in most parts of the world where civilization has been highly developed. In this respect Europe is not unique.

Be that as it may, theology is rooted in culture, sharing its glories and its defects. The missionaries were educated in a scholastic theology, the heritage of the Middle Ages, which was like a huge, solid pyramid of which one could say "always the same" (*semper idem*), which had little awareness of cultures other than its own, and which was confident that it had nothing to learn from anybody. The notions of change, progress, development, which are so familiar to us today, were almost entirely absent from this great structure systematized according to the categories of Aristotle. If dialogue entails a readiness to change (and it does) then this pyramid was ill-suited to dialogue. If dialogue means appreciating the truth and goodness of others, children of this age were ill-equipped for such an undertaking.

And perhaps the weakest point in this theology was its cognitional theory, particularly its views on the objectivity of truth. Of certain scholastics who were fascinated by such objectivity Bernard Lonergan shrewdly observes that "they seem to have thought of truth as so objective as to get along without minds."[1] This is a fair comment. One-sided emphasis on objectivity can lead to a naive realism that regards truth as something "out there" to be looked at. "I see it; so I am right. You do not see it; so you are wrong. And error has no rights. Besides, truth is one. There cannot be two truths. We cannot both be right." How simple!

Now I do not say that all scholastics propounded naive realism in such an extreme and ludicrous way. Aquinas, who is the giant behind scholasticism, certainly did not. But nevertheless it was a way of thinking that predominated in the scholastic theology that formed the missionaries and held sway until the Second Vatican Council. And it rendered dialogue impossible. For how can I authentically dialogue with another if I am basically convinced that he or she is in error? How can I sincerely dialogue with another if I believe that all the truth is on my side while he or she sits sadly in the shadows of ignorance? Far from being open to learn from such persons I will seek only to rescue them from their unhappy plight. I can only sincerely dialogue if I believe that there is some truth and goodness in the person to whom I speak.

But where is the fallacy in naive realism and how is one to get out of this trap? This is a crucial question that sounds simple but is, in fact, quite complex, for it lies at the center of the so-called critical problem that has challenged the finest Western minds from Plato to Kant and from Aristotle to Russell. Here only let me express my own conviction that one must steer a middle course between a naive realism that overemphasizes objectivity to the neglect of the subject and the extreme idealism that denies any objectivity whatsoever. This is the path of moderate realism. And here again I agree with Bernard Lonergan that one comes to this moderate realism not just through reasoning and thinking but through conversion or enlightenment. One must come to the existential realization of what it means to know, and this can be done by reflecting on one's own process of knowing, by analyzing one's interior states of consciousness. "It is not just a question of assenting to a number of true propositions. More basically it is a matter of conversion, of a personal philosophical experience, of moving out of a world of sense and arriving, dazed and disorientated for a while, into a universe of being."[2] Then I can say to myself: "Yes, I do know objective reality, but in a creative way through understanding and judgment."[3]

Now it is easy to see how all this affects a Christian's attitude towards Buddhism and other non-Christian religions. Without this intellectual conversion we may find ourselves incapable of recognizing the truth in other people. And then dialogue may become a pretense, a bland and hypocritical show. Or it may simply grind to a standstill.

On the other hand, if we do come to realize existentially that truth depends upon both the object and the mind we find ourselves radically changed. And one of the conclusions to which we are drawn is that while truth in the mind of God is absolute, eternal and unchanging, *truth as grasped by the human mind is always partial.* Our grasp of eternal truth (about God and the Incarnation and eternal life) is always limited and inadequate. This means that our knowledge can always grow, and at once we are brought to the conclusion that theology is a developing science. The great pyramid collapses and we envisage theology as open-ended, progressing, ongoing and dynamic. Now it is more like a flowing river than a solid pyramid. It is true that God is eternal and immutable, but our knowledge of God is always open to development. And the same holds true for our knowledge of Christ and his mysteries. In this way the royal road to progress through dialogue is thrown open.

For if our grasp of truth is partial, can we not envisage the possibility that there is partial truth in non-Christian religions also? May they not possess aspects of the truth that we have not seen? Is it not possible that they will even cast light on the mystery of God and Christ? And in offering them our share of the truth, must we not be sensitive to the truth they already possess and build on that? As can be readily seen, a sound cognitional theory and a sound approach to truth prepare the way for dialogue. We quickly come to the conclusion that if we wish to grow in truth we must listen to other people.

II

But now let me return to the missionaries. I have spoken mainly about the Catholic missionary effort. The Protestant missionaries who came later had different problems, the chief of which was an extremely fundamentalist approach to the Bible. While there have always been various shades of Protestantism in the West, the Protestant theology that came to the missions tended to regard everything outside the Bible as evil. It took its picture of Asia from a fundamentalist interpretation of the opening chapters of the Epistle to the Romans; non-Christians were the *massa damnata.* With such a theological outlook dialogue becomes impossible.

Having said all this, however, let me repeat that I have been speaking about the prevailing theological climate. Not all the missionaries were naive realists or narrow-minded fundamentalists.

Their native common sense and their inner experience frequently taught them what knowing is. And their faith taught them that God loves all men and women. Indeed, what remains remarkable in the whole missionary enterprise is not the European chauvinism of the missionaries but the fact that so many succeeded in rising above their cultural conditioning to display a profound sympathy for the new cultures they encountered and came to love. One has only to mention the names of Robert de Nobili in India, of Mateo Ricci in China, of Alessandro Valignano in Japan. One has only to read the magnificent letters of the missionaries vividly describing the worlds they encountered. One has only to recall the great Protestant missionaries of the nineteenth and twentieth centuries, outstanding orientalists, who translated the *Tao te Ching*, the *I Ching*, the *Analects of Confucius* and many Buddhist classics. Of the Japanese Protestant mission Notto Thelle writes: "It is a great mistake to regard the missionaries who came to Japan after the Meiji Restoration as narrow-minded preachers without understanding of Japanese culture and religions. In fact the Meiji missionaries were carefully selected people, intelligent, experienced, mature. They approached Japanese culture with interest and wisdom, and became pioneers in many fields of Japanese studies, such as language, literature, geography, botany, meteorology, folk customs, philosophy, Ainu studies . . ."[4]

And so, while it is true, as Notto Thelle points out, that Buddhists violently attacked Christians and Christians answered in kind, glimmerings of authentic dialogue were never absent. Hampered though they were by training and culture, controlled though they were by people who never set foot in Asia, the Christian missionaries nevertheless frequently transcended the limitations of their upbringing to show themselves pioneers in oriental studies and in transcultural thinking.

III

In the years following World War II, Western cultural chauvinism broke down and the West began loudly to challenge its own past. Under the influence of the empirical methodology of science, Western culture began to see itself not as *the* culture but as *one* culture among many. Western youth ran to Asia to don saffron robes, to practice zen and yoga, to learn karate and judo, to write with the brush and to eat with chopsticks. Some missionaries did likewise. Many Asians were astonished and slightly amused. Was this dialogue or was it cultural decline? Put positively, Western youth were beautifully open to other cultures; put negatively, the Western world was disillusioned, floundering, frustrated and rootless.

Some theologians, however, began to take a serious look at the truth and goodness in Hinduism and Buddhism. Like the missionaries of old they often found pearls and jewels; but they considered it a solemn duty to prove that, after all, Christianity was superior. And so we had the famous last chapter pointing out that everything good in the non-Christian religion was fulfilled in the Christian revelation as understood by the Western church. Typical of this approach was Teilhard de Chardin (1881–1955). Undoubtedly he showed penetrating and admirable insight into the religions of Asia; but he always kept protesting that Christianity is optimistic whereas Buddhism is pessimistic, that Christian mysticism exalts the human person whereas Buddhism annihilates the human person, and that the privilege of cultural leadership belongs to the West. To modern ears he sounds chauvinistic. But let us not judge him. Teilhard, for all his futurology, was a child of his time.

Then came the Second Vatican Council (1962–1965). Overnight the Catholic church which had been a Western institution exporting its wares to the East became a world community. Asian and African bishops and theologians assembled in Rome and, with their European and American confreres, acknowledged that the Spirit of God is at work in all peoples and in all religions. Since then, most theologians recognize non-Christian religions as "valid ways." When I say that a religion is a valid way, I simply take it as it is. I do not say it is inferior to my own; I do not even say it is equal to my own. After all, there is no evidence for the statement that all religions are equal. Is not this one of those credos tossed out to keep people happy? So why not leave it unsaid and take people as they are? Only in this way can we address ourselves to sincere and authentic dialogue.

IV

I have spoken about recognizing the *truth* in other religions, and this is a cognitional problem. Closely associated with it is the question of recognizing the *good* in people of other religions and of respecting their conscience. This is an ethical problem. And again it is worth listening to the moving words with which the Second Vatican Council opened its famous *Declaration on Religious Freedom:*

> A sense of the dignity of the human person has been imposing itself more and more deeply on the consciousness of contemporary man. And the demand is increasingly made that men should act on their own judgment, enjoying and making use of a responsible freedom, not driven by coercion but motivated by a sense of duty.[5]

In this way Christians are urged to recognize the judgment and the commitment of other people, even when they differ from their own. Clearly this opens the door to respect and esteem for the committed Buddhist or Hindu or Moslem.

And, of course, this declaration of Vatican II had a history. Already in the nineteenth century John Henry Newman (1801–1890) had spoken prophetically about the supremacy of conscience. His loyalty to Rome is unquestioned, yet it was he who could drink a toast "to the Pope, if you please—still, to conscience first, and to the Pope afterwards."[6] His words shocked some contemporary pious ears; but he was vindicated in his lifetime by being raised to the cardinalate and I myself believe that history will look to him as one of the greatest, perhaps the greatest, theologian of the nineteenth century.

For Newman, Christians of various denominations could find union by a common recognition of the supremacy of conscience. "When Anglicans, Wesleyans, the various Protestant sects in Scotland, and other denominations among us, speak of conscience, they mean what we mean, the voice of God in the nature and heart of man, as distinct from the voice of revelation."[7] And might we not ask if respect for conscience is not a key factor in the union of Buddhists and Christians?

All this points to the truth that while Christians may (indeed *must*) proclaim the gospel of Jesus Christ, they may never exert pressure on anyone but must always have the greatest respect for the human dignity and for the conscience of the person addressed. And furthermore they are urged by Vatican II to respect the good in non-Christian religions.

"All very beautiful," you will say. Yes, I answer. But it demands an ethical conversion of the first magnitude if I am honestly to recognize the good in an apparently rival camp while remaining completely committed to my own religion. I must rise above sectarianism, affirming not "my good" but "the good." I must transcend my ego in a radical way to affirm *the good as it is in itself* and not just *what is apparently good for me*. What a conversion is demanded of anyone who would dialogue with a religion other than his own!

In short, we are now at a point in history where authentic dialogue is possible. This dialogue is in itself a way to enlightenment or conversion. It presupposes, or leads to, an intellectual conversion whereby I sincerely recognize the *truth* in others. It presupposes, or leads to, an ethical conversion whereby I sincerely recognize the *good* in others. Such conversions only come through struggle and pain.

And one final word. Since Vatican II the infant Asian church has grown in wisdom and stature and maturity. Already it is taking upon itself the leadership in dialogue with Buddhism. Already this dialogue is a meeting of Asian Christians with Asian Buddhists. The implications for the universal church of the future are enormous.

The Way of Dialogue

I

In an earlier book I expressed my conviction that any Buddhist-Christian dialogue must be based above all on religious experience and, ideally speaking, upon mysticism. And I further said that the greatest union will be found when Buddhists and Christians meditate together. This, I believe, is true. The deepest union is found in pure and naked faith, by comparison with which theological words and letters are like a candle beside the sun.[8]

Having said this, however, the fact remains that we must eventually use words. Theology is necessary. And the question immediately arises: *Is it possible for Buddhists and Christians to share a common theology?* Or put more bluntly: *Have Buddhists and Christians any common ground?* This question is of primary importance if we are to make progress.

But it is by no means easy to find common ground. Christians may bring up the existence of God or the immortality of the soul, but this evokes no response from Buddhists. Christians may then go one step further and talk about the first principles of metaphysics as enunciated by Aristotle and the scholastics: the principle of contradiction, the principle of causality, the principle of finality. But, alas, these so-called metaphysical first principles will be questioned by Buddhists, as indeed they will be questioned by modern physics. Where, then, do we find common ground?

Here I would like to propose that we can find common ground by working towards a foundational theology based *not upon metaphysics but upon transcendental method*. Even when Buddhists and Christians have different beliefs they can still join hands in a common method that is basically human and leads through conversion or enlightenment to truth and goodness. Concretely, this means fidelity to those transcendental precepts that enshrine the inexorable demands of the human spirit and point the way to human authenticity. Let me, then, speak about these transcendental precepts; and again let me do so as a Christian who wishes to approach Buddhism sympathetically.[9]

II

The first precept is: *Be attentive*. Practically speaking this means *listening*, a process that demands discipline. For psychologists keep telling us that few of us really listen. We feel threatened and we interrupt the other. Or we are preoccupied with our own fears and anxieties. Or we think of what we are going to say next. But the listening I advocate demands a total openness, an attentiveness to our Buddhist brothers and sisters—to what they say, to what they really mean, to their religious experience, to their art, to their tradition, to their history.

However, if dialogue simply meant listening to, and learning from, the other it would be relatively easy. Difficulty arises because while listening to the other I must also listen to myself. I must listen to the Holy Spirit, the *Magister Internus*, who speaks to my heart; and I must also listen to the voices of Jesus, of Paul, of Augustine, of the whole Christian community. And because I am listening to these two choruses I will begin to ask questions. Under the influence of Buddhism I may ask questions Christians have never asked before. I may find myself opening up areas of consciousness that previously were dormant. And this is painful, painful, painful, because all expansion of consciousness entails suffering.[10]

But through this questioning I will come to insight in fulfillment of the second transcendental precept which is: *Be intelligent.* I come to a deeper understanding of the truth.

But insights are plentiful and do not constitute knowledge until I sift them out and make a statement of objective truth. In doing this I obey the third transcendental precept which is: *Be reasonable.* But here again I may feel tension and conflict in the attempt to reconcile a new statement of truth that I have learned from Buddhism with the truth I already have in my Christian tradition. For I am entering new and unchartered territory; I am attempting to integrate new elements of truth into my consciousness. This is a lonely journey in which I cannot expect too much sympathy from my fellow Christians who are rooted in the established order. For they feel desperately insecure when confronted with change. And, of course, the suffering of integrating new data of consciousness is something they can do without. The pioneer in dialogue, like the prophet, is not recognized in his or her own country.

But there is yet another transcendental precept: *Be responsible.* In obedience to this I recognize the good in another religion. And this can be the shock that leads to enlightenment. Such was the experience of Charles de Foucauld (1858–1916) who underwent a profound conversion when he encountered the mysticism of the Moslems in North Africa—a conversion to his own latent Christianity. And did not Jesus wish to effect a similar conversion in his listeners when he drew their attention to the holiness of the good Samaritan, the faith of the Roman centurion and the goodness of others outside the fold? The vision of holiness in another religion can lead to a conversion within one's own.

The final precept is the most important: *Be committed.* This means that I must be committed to truth wherever I see it. And so, while I am committed to the truth I discover in Buddhism, I integrate it with the Christian truth which is mine by baptism.

Let me here pause for a moment to say that I cannot agree with those who claim that for successful dialogue I must temporarily suspend my commitment to my own religion. Nothing could be further from the truth. Even if it were possible to suspend my commitment (and I believe it is not possible) I should not do so, because it is precisely this commitment that enlightens me about the truth of my own religion. Remember Anselm's *Crede ut intelligas: Believe that you may understand: Be committed that you may understand.* Through commitment with its unrestricted love, the truths of faith unintelligible to the unbeliever become intelligible to the one who believes. Consequently, if I suspend my commitment I lose my roots and find myself adrift with nothing to share.

Now all this is important, because one who dialogues may be tempted to compromise or water down his own truth in the specious belief that this is an ecumenical procedure. Or he may be tempted to flirt with another religion and end up committed neither to that religion nor to his own. This is an aberration stemming from infidelity to the transcendental precept: *Be committed.*

III

In the above I have spoken principally about the Christian approach to Buddhism. But dialogue is by definition a two-way exchange; it also entails a sharing on the part of Christians and a listening on the part of Buddhists. And so I must ask: Will Buddhists accept the transcendental method I have outlined?

Obviously only Buddhists themselves can answer this. But let me tentatively advance some reasons why this methodology might be in harmony with Buddhist belief.

The first precept was *be attentive,* and I need hardly say that attentive listening is deeply rooted in Buddhism. Indeed the well-known Buddhist *mindfulness* is precisely this. One way of practicing meditation is to listen to every sound—to the flow of the river, the wind in the trees, the rain on the roof. It is said that the Bodhisattva Kannon got enlightenment just by listening. Moreover Buddhism sets great store not only on listening to external reality but on listening to myself and on asking the question: Who is listening? Again, the oriental master listens with the utmost alertness to his disciple—not only to the disciple's words but, more importantly, to his body language. For him the throat talks, the hands talk, the breath talks, and above all the eyes talk. And he is very, very attentive. All this makes me think that the first transcendental precept, *be attentive*, is preeminently practiced in Buddhism.

The second precept was *be intelligent*, and I spoke about the insight that comes from asking questions. And here again is a pattern of experience found in Buddhism. Writing about the *koan*, Dr. D. T. Suzuki stresses the importance of what he calls *the spirit of enquiry*. One must keep asking, asking, asking, until the breakthrough takes place and one gets the sudden flash of enlightenment. Here is remarkable fidelity to the precept *be intelligent*. [11]

Problems arise, however, when we come to the third transcendental precept, *be reasonable*. Here, it will be remembered, I objectify my experience and make a statement to the effect that such and such really is so. And this, I suspect, would make a zen Buddhist pause. Because, as everyone knows, zen Buddhism constantly inveighs against the discriminating intellect, against words and letters, against any kind of theory, against statements either of affirmation or denial. This, then, would seem to be a hurdle for anyone who would propose this method to Buddhists. [12]

And let me first say that I have the greatest sympathy with the Buddhist stance. Profoundly contemplative, zen appreciates the beauty of the sunset, the floating clouds, the cascading waterfall, the experience of enlightenment. And it feels that objective statements fail to capture these experiences and even cheapen them. And so Buddhists prefer to remain silent. Or they will write a poem or paint a picture or express themselves through body language. As I have said, I understand this stance, which is not unlike that of the Christian mystics. These latter feel that words and letters are totally inadequate to express the reality they have experienced, and so they prefer to say nothing.

But it is one thing to say that words are inadequate and it is another thing to say they are false. Inadequate though they may be, they have some value; and great Buddhist thinkers and scholars have used them, and still use them, to make statements and to elaborate profound philosophy. That is why I would hope that this third transcendental precept might be acceptable in the Buddhist world.

Besides, there is one more point to be considered. If Buddhists reject words and letters and objective statements, this is largely because such objectivization smacks of the dualism the Buddhist tradition abhors, a dualism that seems to destroy the unitive experience of enlightenment. But is this really so? Is the judgment really dualistic? Here we are back again to the critical problem with all its intricacies. For if I am a naive realist who looks on the judgment as a statement about something that is "out there," then objective statements are radically dualistic. But if I can get out of the trap of naive realism by understanding my own process of thinking, if I can steer the midway path between naive realism and Kantian idealism, then I will grasp something of what is meant by "self-transcendence." I will come to see that in the judgment I am one with the object while remaining myself. And, in consequence, I can confidently assert that objective judgments are not simply dualistic.

Now all this, far from being empty theory, has the widest ramifications. Popular writers on Buddhism maintain the old attack on "conceptualization," or they flagellate the "discriminating intellect," or they throw contempt on any kind of theory; but the real problem is that they have had no intellectual conversion and do not know what knowing is. Underlying their assertions is the naive realism that thinks judgments and statements divide and split things up in a dualistic way.

The conclusion I wish to draw is that the formation of judgments is quite compatible with the experience of enlightenment and that, in fact, many highly enlightened people make judgments and statements. The charge of dualism cannot be leveled against the third transcendental precept, *be reasonable*.

The fourth precept, *be responsible*, which tells us to recognize the values and commitment of others, is not, I believe, a problem for Buddhism which from time immemorial has been an extremely tolerant religion.

The final precept is *be committed*. Anyone who has had even a little contact with practicing Buddhists knows of their total commitment to the Buddha, the *dharma* and the *sangha*. He or she knows of the Buddhist vows to extinguish all passions and to save all sentient beings. He or she knows of the determination of the zen monk to "break through" even if it costs him his life. And so we find in Buddhism an earthshaking commitment to truth together with the belief that salvation is found through the great grasp of truth called enlightenment.

Speaking about non-Christian religions, the Second Vatican Council said simply and directly that "the Catholic church rejects nothing which is true and holy in these religions."[13] And in this way the Council encouraged non-Christians to be committed to the goodness and truth they already have. But in dialogue, just as Christians integrate Buddhist insights into their Christian outlook, so Buddhists will integrate the truth they learn from Christianity and be committed to it. In this way their commitment will be increasingly enriched.

IV

And so I tentatively propose this methodology as a way to mutual union, development and enrichment. I propose it with a certain amount of confidence because I believe that *something like this is already happening*. Buddhists and Christians are beginning to listen to one another, to understand one another, to appreciate one another, to love one another. And as they do so, they reflect on themselves, examining the place where they stand. Moreover Christians who have never even talked to Buddhists are integrating Buddhist ideas into their lives—and the same holds true for Buddhists faced with Christianity. This is particularly true in Buddhist countries like Japan, and in time it will hold true for the West.

But I have no intention of idealizing things. There are hurdles and obstacles, some of which seem insuperable. Let me then select some of the major problems, frankly admitting that in many cases they admit of no logical solution.

Problems of Dialogue

I

The first problem is that both Christianity and Buddhism are missionary religions. Christians are committed to proclaim the gospel in obedience to the words of Jesus: "Go therefore and make disciples of all nations . . ." (Matt. 28:19). Buddhists are committed to work for the salvation of all sentient beings in obedience to their vow: "Sentient beings are innumerable: I vow to save them all." And so while

Christians have always courageously carried the gospel to the ends of the earth, Buddhists with equal courage have spread the *dharma*. And in both cases they have believed that their teaching is the way of salvation.

How, then, does this square with dialogue? Can there be dialogue between two religions pledged to make converts? Must they not necessarily come into a conflict, which makes dialogue a sham and a hypocrisy? Or if they do compromise and talk, will not this water down the basic teaching of both religions—will it not mean that the fire of Christian zeal and the ardor of Buddhist determination burn out and die?

This is indeed a formidable problem. But let me suggest some reflections that may point to a solution.

The first concerns the motivation behind missionary activity. As I have already pointed out, much of the old mission theology was based on the I-am-right-and-you-are-wrong frame of mind bolstered by a naive realism. Added to this was the commonly held belief that explicit knowledge of the gospel was necessary for salvation. Without this faith and without baptism of water the nonbeliever was in danger of eternal damnation. Hence the famous prayer of Xavier about hell filling with the very souls whom Christ had come to save. Anyone reciting this prayer with fervor, it was thought, would inevitably be filled with zeal to spread the gospel with the utmost rapidity. Xavier himself baptized until his exhausted arm fell wearily to his side.

Now all this theology has been rethought, and since Vatican II no serious theologian doubts the goodness of non-Christians. This is particularly true of theologians who have met non-Christians face to face and have dialogued with them. They know that the task of missionaries is not to save them from hell. But if so, what *is* their task? What is their motivation? Why are they impelled to spread the gospel?

I myself believe that true missionary zeal is based not on the anguishing fear that people will be damned but on love for Christ and love for Christ's message, which one wishes to share with people whom one has come to love. And precisely because one loves these people one will appreciate the good things they have—and one will never force or threaten or put pressure on them. One will always maintain the greatest respect for their human dignity and human liberty, all the more so because one realizes that no human being can give faith. "I planted, Apollos watered, but God gave the growth" wrote Paul (1 Cor. 3:6). The role of the missionary is to plant and water, leaving the rest to God.

Ideally speaking, the missionary is one who loves Christ so much that he wishes to spread his name and share the good news of the gospel. With Paul he exclaims, "The love of Christ impels us . . ." (2 Cor. 5:14, DOUAY-RHEIMS VERSION). With Paul he cries, "For necessity is laid upon me. Woe to me if I do not preach the gospel" (1 Cor. 9:16). As if to say: "I cannot do otherwise; I cannot but spread the good news." With Paul he can quote Isaiah, "How beautiful are the feet of those who preach the good news (Rom. 10:15). With Paul he sees a vision in the night: a man of Macedonia beseeching him and saying, "Come over to Macedonia and help us" (Acts 16:9). And so he proclaims the word with Pauline power and enthusiasm.

In short, the authentic missionary is called to be a mystic—in love with Jesus and his word and with people. And I believe that something similar can be said of the Buddhist who spreads the *dharma*. Obviously it is not for me to expound Buddhist missionary theology (this must be left to a Buddhist thinker), but perhaps I can express my belief that the authentic Buddhist is more committed to the Buddha and to the *dharma* than to the fear that people will be lost if they do not embrace Buddhist teaching.

Now it seems to me that if we purify our motivation, basing it more and more upon love, we will lose nothing of our zeal. For who will deny that love accomplishes more than fear? Furthermore (and this is a relevant point just here) we will not hurt one another. I can say from my own experience that I am happy to hear Buddhists speak of their enlightenment; I am happy to hear them expound the *dharma*, provided they do not attempt to *force* it upon me. Similarly I have found that Buddhists are happy to hear about Christ, about Paul's meeting with Christ on the road to Damascus, about our Christian experience—provided no attempt is made to superimpose it upon them or to pressure them into some belief they cannot accept.

And so, dialogue need mean no lessening of missionary zeal. Both Christians and Buddhists can (and should) be left free to speak clearly and loudly about the message or about the person they love. And as for clashing with one another, this will not happen if Christians and Buddhists are intellectually and morally converted. For then they will freely recognize the truth and goodness in one another.

But here let me pause honestly and realistically to say that few people, either Christian or Buddhist, are totally converted. We all have our dark and unconverted parts; and so I believe that there will always be rivalry and tension. But even this can spur us on to an ever deepening conversion of mind and heart and to a growing friendship. I myself believe that dialogue will be one important aspect of missionary activity in the future. Without pressure of any kind Christians and Buddhists will be free to teach the gospel and the *dharma* to one another and to all they meet.

II

Following closely upon this is a second problem, namely that of triumphalism. Is not one who is deeply convinced of the truth of his or her own religion certain to lord it over others with a "holier than thou" attitude? And is not this particularly true of Jews and Christians who claim to be the chosen people, who speak of "divine election"? How can one dialogue in terms of equality when one claims to be specially chosen by God?

In an interesting article in *The Ecumenist* Rabbi Gunther Plaut speaks of recent Jewish struggles with the notion of Israel's divine election.[14] After facing squarely the ecumenical difficulties of such a stance and discussing various recent attempts to modify it, or water it down, or explain it away, he concludes that the Jewish people cannot authentically deny this central teaching of their scriptures. And the same, I believe, holds true for Christians. They, too, hear as addressed to themselves the words of Yahweh: "I have called you by name, you are mine" (Isa. 43:1). With Paul they believe that they were "chosen in him before the foundation of the world" (Eph. 1:4). Now I think that neither Jews nor Christians should compromise on this doctrine. For deeply interiorized, it leads not to triumphalism but to humility, and that for two reasons.

The first is that we have no objective proof that we are chosen. It is all a question of faith—something we believe because we believe—and in this sense it is very subjective. When we glory in this kind of truth we are glorying in our weakness and in the Pauline sense we are really fools. This is far from triumphalism.

Secondly, ours must be the attitude of people who know that they are the unworthy recipients of a beautiful treasure. Both Jew and Christian know that Israel is chosen not for any merits of its own but because God loves: "It was not because you were more in number than any other people that the Lord set his love upon you and chose you, for you were the fewest of all peoples; but it is because the Lord loves you, and is keeping the oath which he swore to your fathers . . ." (Deut. 7:7,8). The humility of these words is reechoed in the cry of Peter: "Depart from me, for I am a sinful man, O Lord" (Luke 5:8). Great grace leads to a sense of unworthiness which is the very antithesis of triumphalism.

On this point the Japanese Carmelite, Ichiro Okumura, makes some interesting comments. He was dialoguing on Japanese television with the well-known Zen Master Sogen Omori, when the latter observed that Christians who are interested in zen seem to have lost confidence in their own faith. Father Okumura replied by distinguishing between a certain *confidence*, which should be lost, and a *conviction*, which should be retained:

> If the literal meaning of "confidence" is to believe in oneself, as the Chinese ideographs indicate, then it should not be the attitude of religious people to act on the basis of "self," which is not worthy of such trust. If religion is ultimately a realization of one's own emptiness, folly and poverty, and hence a reliance on God, the only One worthy of reliance, then such "confidence" is quite incompatible with genuine religion. If, unfortunately, many religious leaders and believers seem to have strong and unshakable "confidence" in their own religion, is it not a kind of "confidence" which ought to be abandoned, an unhealthy overconfidence? Instead, *it should be a "conviction" that should never be lost*—an unshakable faith in the religious truth to which we submit ourselves. "Confidence" in religion does not stem from "self" but is faith in *God*, to whom we devote ourselves completely.[15]

Father Okumura goes on to observe that triumphalism is no prerogative of Christianity but is found everywhere. "This arrogance is not restricted to Christianity, but can be found in Hinduism and Buddhism as well, both religions which are supposedly marked by tolerance of others. Unfortunately it is almost impossible for human beings to free themselves completely from their egos."[16]

This is very perceptive. It lets us see that we are all tempted to triumphalism. We are all tempted to think ourselves better than others. It is the old problem of pride. But let us also remember that this is the temptation of beginners. Truly enlightened persons, be they Christian or Buddhist, simply and humbly reverence others. "In humility count others better than yourselves" wrote Paul (Phil. 2:3). And his advice is helpful for Jew and gentile and anyone else.

III

The third and principal problem is in the area of Christology and touches upon the person of Jesus himself. Who was Jesus Christ? "Who do men say that the Son of Man is?" (Matt. 16:13). This great mystery lies at the heart of Christianity and at the heart of Christianity's relationship with other religions. Let me put the problem clearly. The Christian is committed to believe that Jesus is the way, the truth and the life and that no one goes to the Father except through him (John 14:6). He is committed to believe that Jesus is the mediator of grace to all men and that there is no other name under heaven by which men are saved (Acts 4:12). And it is difficult to see how there could be any compromise on these points.

Obviously Buddhists cannot accept Jesus in this way, for here we are at the heart of Christian faith. But in dialogue it is not possible, nor even necessary, that we agree on all points. Let me, then, submit some considerations that may promote mutual understanding.

The first consideration is that we find more union with Buddhists when we move from the objective to the subjective order. Concretely we do this by distinguishing between Jesus Christ as *the mediator of grace* and Jesus Christ as *the mediator of meaning*. I believe that Jesus Christ is the mediator of grace to the whole human race, but he is not the mediator of meaning to Buddhists or to other people who do not believe in him. They find meaning in their own set of symbols—in the Buddha and the *dharma* and whatever it may be. In short, we can say that Christ mediates *meaning* to the Christian and the Buddha mediates *meaning* to the Buddhist. I believe this is something we will all agree on.

Again, Buddhists and Christians can be united at the level of faith—particularly at the level of pure faith, naked faith, mystical faith. About this I have written elsewhere and need not repeat myself here. Only let me say that while we can be united in the subjective order, once we pass to the objective order asking about "faith in what" or "faith in whom" we clearly part company and must simply recognize one another's conscience. For Christians it is once more a question of Christology. But let me again quote Ichiro Okumura. Father Okumura appeals to Chinese philosophy. The human religious consciousness, which is the same everywhere, is the *yin;* Christ is the *yang.* People of all religions are united by reason of the *yin;* but Christ, the *yang,* "is unique, absolute, historical reality, and so Christianity cannot be equated with other religions. In other words, here the absoluteness and uniqueness of Christianity stands out in bold relief."[17]

And so he concludes:

> The essence of Christianity must be found in *Christ himself.* It is not found in the religious character of Christians. Christ himself has something that is not included in the idea of so-called religion. Religion is said to be "the relationship between God and man." This religious relationship is revealed as the greatest historical fact in the mystery of Christ's incarnation, because Christ is the reality wherein God becomes man. Christ is not a religion, that is, the ultimate *teaching* of human life. He is not a teaching but a "reality." Historical protofact of two thousand years ago becomes endless historico-religious reality in Christianity and in the church. In this sense, Christianity is meta-religious, meta-spacial, meta-chronological, historical divino-human reality.[18]

This is a courageous statement of the Christian position, and it is a statement that, I believe, must be made. But I think it can be developed by distinguishing between the Risen Jesus whom Teilhard de Chardin calls "the cosmic Christ" and the historical Jesus who walked by the Sea of Galilee and climbed the mountain to pray. This latter Jesus was, like Paul, a Hebrew—he spoke as a Jew, thought as a Jew and acted as a Jew. But the Risen Lord, while being the same Jesus, belongs to all cultures and all peoples. This means that all cultures can claim him as their own and all religions can tell us something about who he is. This belief in the transcultural nature of the Risen Jesus has already appeared in the art and sculpture of many nations and races but the theological elaboration is far from complete. What can be said is that Christology is developing and that Buddhism may well throw light on the mystery of the Risen Jesus.

In view of all this, some theologians have called non-Christians "anonymous Christians"—men and women who possess the grace of

Christ without knowing that they do so. This is ingeniously logical and, as an attempt to solve the old problem of the salvation of the non-Christian, it may have had some validity. But it does not help dialogue. After all, what Christian would like to be called an anonymous Buddhist? Should we not have more sensitivity for the feelings of those with whom we dialogue? I myself would suggest that we refrain from pushing logic to its ultimate point and learn to live with the paradox and the tension. On the one hand Christ is the savior of all people; on the other hand many good people who do not know Christ overflow with sanctity. If we abandon attempts at a logical solution to this baffling problem we may come up with an intuitive answer like the response to the zen koan. And then we will really understand and rejoice. Then we will understand something about enlightenment.

IV

A final problem may be phrased as follows: Is it possible to be a Buddhist and a Christian at the same time? This question is all the more meaningful in view of the fact that some Christians now practise zen assiduously and wish to incorporate the treasures of Buddhism into the Christian life.

While I myself believe that Buddhism and Christianity have many good things to offer one another, I also believe that both religions have their own identities and that a merging of the two is not possible at this point in history. And I think that most authentic Buddhists will agree with me on this point.[19]

For the essence of the Buddhist commitment is summed up in the triple invocation that echoes through Buddhist literature and through Buddhist life:

> I put my trust in the Buddha
> I put my trust in the *dharma*
> I put my trust in the *sangha*

Here the Buddha is the true self, the *dharma* is the great collection of Buddhist teachings and the *sangha* is the Buddhist community. In committing themselves totally to this triple treasure Buddhists believe that they will find liberation and salvation.

Christians, on the other hand, have their own triple treasure:

I put my trust in Jesus
I put my trust in the gospel
I put my trust in the church

And through this total commitment Christians hope for salvation and for eternal life.

Now obviously Jesus is not the Buddha, the gospel is not the *dharma* and the church is not the *sangha*. While the Christian has the greatest respect for the Buddhist treasures, while he believes that he can learn profound lessons from them, he believes that salvation comes through faith in Jesus. And similarly while the Buddhist may have the greatest respect for Jesus and the gospel, he believes that salvation comes from commitment to his own treasures. In short, while through dialogue Christians and Buddhists may love one another and while their ultimate goal, as it lies beyond the cloud of unknowing, may be the same, their basic concrete commitment is different. It is true that some Christians have attained to an enlightenment that is recognized as such by a Buddhist master; but the authentic Christian evaluates this experience in a different way from the Buddhists. He believes that salvation comes not through Buddhist enlightenment but through faith in Jesus Christ.[20]

V

Where the dialogue is going we do not know, but I would hazard the guess that it is leading to a revolution in Christian spirituality. Already we see the rise of a new Christian meditation movement. Already we begin to realize that one can pray not just with the mind but also with the body and the breathing. Already Christians who dialogue with Buddhists are discovering that levels of consciousness previously dormant are opening up to the presence of God. Already it becomes apparent that Christian mysticism is in its infancy and that the mysticism of the future will outshine in splendor anything that has existed in the past. We are experiencing a great leap forward in consciousness that will dominate the religious experience of the future.

NOTES

1. Bernard Lonergan, *A Second Collection* (Philadelphia: Westminster Press; London: Darton, Longman and Todd, 1974), p. 71. Lonergan speaks here of "theologians from the days of Suarez, de Lugo, and Bañez." These theologians were influential in the seminaries where the future missionaries studied.
2. Ibid., p. 79.
3. See the scholastic adage: *Quidquid recipitur per modum recipientis recipitur*, i.e., "Whatever is received (known) is received (known) according to the mode of the knower." This emphasizes the creative role of the knower in all knowledge.
4. Notto Thelle, "From Anathema to Dialogue: Buddhist-Christian Relations in Japan," *Japanese Religions* (Kyoto), December 1978.
5. *The Documents of Vatican II*, ed. Walter M. Abbott, (New York: America Press, 1966), p. 675. The Council further adds: "The truth cannot impose itself except by virture of its own truth, as it makes its entrance into the mind at once quietly and with power" (p.677).
6. John Coulson, *Newman and the Common Tradition* (England: Oxford University Press, 1970), p. 151.
7. Ibid., p. 152.
8. In my book, *The Inner Eye of Love* (New York: Harper & Row; London: Collins, 1978) I distinguish between faith and belief, and state that Buddhists and Christians are most closely united at the level of that pure and naked faith which is mystical experience.
9. These transcendental precepts are the basis of Bernard Lonergan's method. I will speak more about them and how they originate in the next chapter.
10. Raymond Panikkar in *The Intrareligious Dialogue* (New York: Paulist Press, 1978) distinguishes between an *interreligious* dialogue and an *intrareligious* dialogue. The latter is "an inner dialogue within myself, an encounter in the depth of my personal religiousness, having met another religious experience on that very intimate level" (p.40). Let me here add that one of the great religious dialogues of all time was between Aguinas and Aristotle. Aquinas was less interested in interpreting the mind of Aristotle according to the norms of modern higher criticism than in rethinking the Christian faith in the light of Aristotle.
11. See D. T. Suzuki, *Essays in Zen Buddhism: Second Series* (London: Rider, 1970), p. 95 ff.
12 There is a zen saying: "In our sect there are no written letters to be set down, no words and phrases to be known, no delusion to be freed from, no enlightenment to be obtained."
13 *The Documents of Vatican II*, p. 662.
14. Rabbi Gunther Plaut, "Jewish-Catholic Dialogue on Divine Election," *The Ecumenist*, November–December 1978.
15. Ichiro Okumura, O.C.D., "Dialogue with Other Religions," *The Third Asian Regional Meeting of the Federation of Asian Bishops* (Tokyo), March 27, 1979.
16. Ibid.
17. Ibid. Okumura maintains that Christianity is a religion of a special kind: "Christianity is, so to speak, a compound of Christ and religion. First, Christianity is basically identical with other religions in that its religious character constitutes it as a religion, and so it should be. This is the *causa materialis* in scholastic philosophy. Secondly, the unique, absolute existence of Christ, which is not found in any other religion, is the *causa formalis seu exemplaris.*"
18. Ibid.
19. Dialogue with Buddhism is quite different from dialogue between Christians. The

latter aim at complete union in accordance with the prayer of Jesus that his disciples be one. Buddhists and Christians, on the other hand, do not now aim at becoming one religion.

20. I believe that faith in Jesus Christ is an enlightenment of another kind.

2

Self-Realization

MODERN MEN AND women are greatly interested in their inner world, in their deepest self, in their personal identity. We want to *know* ourselves, and so we ask: "Who am I? Where do I come from? Where are my roots? What is at the core of my being?" We want to *realize* ourselves, and so we ask: "How can I become my true self? How can I be truly human? How can I be authentic?"

And, of course, the twin search for self-knowledge and self-realization extends over a whole lifetime. It is a search that is full of pitfalls and conflict and suffering. But it is worth while. Indeed, our deepest instincts tell us that it is the only thing that is worth while; to realize ourselves is the great illumination, the great enlightenment, the great goal.[1]

In Modern Thought

I

In the search for self-knowledge, a certain methodology is quietly evolving—a methodology that demands deep reflection on self. In psychology one immediately thinks of Carl Rogers, who invites us to reflect on our feelings, be they positive or negative. We are asked to reflect on, and be aware of, our joy and our fear, our tenderness and our anger, our hope and our frustration, our cheerfulness and our depression, our trust and our guilt, our sexual desires and our sexual fears. Reflecting on these feelings I come to recognize, differentiate, "appropriate" and "own" them. Now I objectivize them, talk about them, accept them, control them, and lead a life that is increasingly integrated, increasingly enriched, increasingly human. And all this is done in the context of interpersonal relations. Because it is in relationship with others that I come to know myself and to realize myself.

And a somewhat similar methodology can be applied to my acts of knowledge and love. Here again I can reflect on self and come to know objectively what it is to know and to love. Such is the approach of Bernard Lonergan, who can write of his great book *Insight:*

"The first eight chapters . . . are a series of five-finger exercises inviting the reader to discover in himself and for himself just what happens when he understands. My aim is to help people experience in themselves understanding, advert to the experience, name and identify it, and recognize it when it recurs. My aim, I surmise, is parallel to Carl Rogers's aim of inducing his clients to advert to the feelings they experience but do not advert to, distinguish, name, identify, recognize."[2]

In short, Lonergan is asking people to discover who they are in order to help them be themselves. At first, his ideal and his presentation may sound dull and drab—a fitting pursuit for bald scholars and bearded philosophers. But in fact it is not so. The understanding of one's understanding is even more thrilling than the Rogerian reflection on feeling. It brings the profound and liberating intellectual conversion I spoke about in the last chapter. It can be an earthshaking enlightenment.

Carl Rogers and Bernard Lonergan speak principally of the conscious mind (though in this area the dividing line between conscious and unconscious is blurred), but equally significant is the discovery of the unconscious mind with its many mansions. The world has moved rapidly since Freud and Jung broke through to the subliminal levels of the mind; and now the ordinary person is constantly invited to look into the depths of his or her unconscious with its suppressed fears and buried anguish. And if we follow Jung we are invited to look even deeper into the collective unconscious, into the archetypal world of bewitching beauty and frightening evil.

And again the method is reflection on self. Now one reflects on one's dreams or daydreams. Or one can reflect on the contents of the unconscious through Christian contemplation or through meditation of the kind that is now called oriental. For in such meditation, data from the unconscious surges into consciousness and appears before the eyes of the mind. One can objectivize all this with a counselor or by writing a journal or even by some artistic pursuit such as painting or calligraphy. And all this is therapeutic. Jung, who was a doctor, saw it as a process through which the split between the conscious and the unconscious mind is healed. Through reflection, our unconscious slowly becomes conscious and we come to understand and accept it. We come to own it and appropriate it; we become increasingly human and whole.

In addition to reflecting on our feelings and our cognition and our unconscious, however, we can reflect on our religious experience. This was encouraged by St. Ignatius of Loyola (1491–1556) who in this respect was a man ahead of his time, for he would have people reflect on what is happening during their prayer and during their life with God. He wants them to be aware of the consolations and desolations, of the light and the darkness, of the peace and the turmoil, of the gentle movements of grace and the disturbing movements of evil. "We must carefully observe the whole course of our thoughts," he writes. "If the beginning and middle and end of the course of thoughts are wholly good and directed to what is entirely right, it is a sign that they are from the good angel."[3] What astonishing inner vigilance Ignatius demands! It is as though he were saying: "Watch your thoughts! Watch your feelings! Reflect on yourself!"

I have already said that Ignatius was in advance of his times. The self-reflective dimension of his *Spiritual Exercises* was not well understood until today, when we see a great resurgence of interest in the privately directed retreat, where the role of the spiritual director is to help the exercitant reflect on self, objectivize his or her religious experience and see where he or she is going.

II

Now about the whole matter of reflection on self I would like to make two observations. The first is that there is a world of difference between *experiencing* a thing and *knowing* it. We can experience all kinds of feelings in our conscious mind without knowing them. And this, Carl Rogers rightly says, is one of our basic problems. We can know all kinds of things without knowing what knowing is. And this, Lonergan rightly says, is one of our basic problems. Our unconscious mind may be filled with disturbing complexes or inspiring movements and we may not even know that they are there. And this, Jung rightly says, is one of our basic problems. And again we can have all kinds of religious experiences and be quite incapable of recognizing them. And this, Ignatius rightly says, is one of our basic problems. Because in so far as we do not know ourselves we do not own or "appropriate" what is within us and we are that much less human. In this context Abraham Maslow writes that when he began to study peak experiences he thought that such experiences were rare, but as his study progressed he found that all kinds of people have peak experiences without even recognizing them. I believe that something like this happened to those two disciples going to Emmaus. They met Jesus on the road and thought little of it. Only later did they *awaken* (and this I call a glimpse of self-realization) to what was in their own hearts and exclaim: "Did not our hearts burn within us while he talked to us on the road . . . ?" (Luke 24:32).

But I need not labor this point. Only let me say that I personally have met people who claim that they have no religious experience and even no faith, when in fact all they need to do is to reflect on themselves. If they do so, they discover hidden treasures in the fields of their own souls.

The second point I wish to make is that this process of self-knowledge can be accompanied by great joy and great suffering. There is tremendous joy in discovering and understanding the truth within oneself. But one can also be traumatically faced with problems that were previously hidden. It is not always joyful to come face to face with one's relationship with father or mother. It is not always joyful to be faced with one's own sexual identity. It is not always joyful to see one's wounds. And it is even more painful to come face to face with the murky shadow of evil that hovers over us. If we have deep faith in God and encouraging help from other people, this can be a most healing and liberating experience. But even then it is painful and perilous. And we need to have great compassion toward ourselves.

III

From all that has been said it will be clear that we are not born ourselves—we become ourselves. And this does not happen in a few days or weeks or months. It is the work of a lifetime and reaches its climax only in death, which is the last stage in growth. For we know that just as the body grows, so also does the psyche. During the first part of our life, growth is effected principally by personal effort as we strive for goals and achievement. During the second period of life we will only grow if we master the great art of *wu-wei* or non-action—learning to let growth take place so that we can develop to our fullness as persons.

Nor is growth automatic. Some of the seed sown by the sower falls on rocky ground and dies; other seed falls by the wayside and is trampled under foot; other seed grows up only to be choked by thorns. As bodily growth can be stunted and blocked, so also can growth in the psyche. And so we are brought to ask about the laws of growth—are there such laws and, if so, how can they be formulated?

To answer this let me once again appeal to the self-reflective method I have been speaking about. If I reflect upon my knowledge, my love and my religious experience, I come to understand the process by which I authentically know and love; and, moreover, I come to experience existentially that there are in this process certain fundamental laws I must obey if I want to be authentically human. These are the transcendental precepts that tell me to be attentive, to be intelligent, to be reasonable, to be responsible, to be committed. These are, I believe, inexorable laws of human nature, but one has to discover them within oneself, and one does so by analysis of one's own inner states in the way I have described. When I obey these laws I am following the good advice Polonius in *Hamlet* gave to his son Laertes: "This above all, to thine own self be true . . ."

But obedience to these laws is not to be taken for granted. We all, alas, have moments when we are inattentive, stupid, unreasonable, irresponsible and hate-filled. And if these moments become the pattern of our lives we find ourselves on the downward road that leads to inauthenticity, a road that leads to hatred of self—not to self-realization but to self-destruction. Here we are at the very center of the human conflict.

However, if I sincerely strive for authenticity I find that in fidelity to the transcendental precepts I transcend myself. Yes, *I find myself by transcending myself*—by going beyond. I transcend myself intellectually when I make objective statements and understand what objectivity is; I transcend myself ethically when I choose the good rather than the pleasant; I transcend myself religiously when I am totally committed or when I fall in love without restriction. And so I am faced with the shocking paradox of human life and of the gospel— that he who loses himself finds himself. *Self-realization is found in self-transcendence.*

This is of the greatest importance for a modern world in which so many people are locked up in themselves—incarcerated by a narrow little ego that refuses to die. "How to get out of prison?" you ask. "By fidelity to the transcendental precepts and in particular by loving others and being loved by them," I reply. If I do this I come to realize that the other is a mirror in which I see myself. I discover my true self in him or in her or in them. And I also am a mirror in which I find them and in which they find themselves.

IV

Jung was deeply aware of human nature's thrust towards self-realization; and he called it *individuation*, a process that ordinarily begins in the middle period of life when people start to ask questions about meaning. But Jung, that wise old sage, saw that this process of self-realization could only take place effectively within a religious framework. Hence his constant and growing preoccupation with religion West and East, a preoccupation that earned him the criticism and disdain of many of his contemporaries but earns him growing respect today. But why did Jung look to religion?

I believe he saw clearly that one does not come to self-realization without a set of symbols or, in his terminology, without a myth. There is a Buddhist myth, a Hindu myth, a Moslem myth, a Jewish myth, a Christian myth, and all of these promote psychic growth, leading the believer to the great realities and truths that lie at the depths of his or her unconscious. Jung found his own myth in alchemy. But to this Jungian reason for the necessity of religion let me add a couple of corollaries.

The first is that anyone who seriously embarks on the search for the true self needs faith. He or she needs to believe that there is indeed a true self (a fact that empirical psychology cannot verify) and that the ultimate thing within us is good. Without this faith there always remains the danger that one will be strangled by the snakes or gobbled up by the wild beasts that haunt the paths leading to the core of one's being. Only the torch of faith can enlighten this perilous way and keep us safe.

The second corollary is that we do not, and cannot, come to self-realization by our own efforts. We need the help of grace. Such is the teaching of Pure Land Buddhism, which is built upon *tariki*, the power of another. Such is the teaching of Christianity, whose founder said: "Apart from me you can do nothing" (John 15:5). Such is the teaching of some transpersonal psychologists who speak not, indeed, about grace but about the energies of the universe to which one must always remain open. Put in Christian terms, the love that leads to self-realization and self-transcendence is not something we drum up at will. Rather is it the gift offered to the human race by its author. He it is who calls us to love. And it is in responding to this call that I transcend myself, go beyond my little ego and find my true self. It is in responding to this love that I lose myself to find myself in the ecstasy of the cry: "Abba! Father!"

V

In all that has been said I have spoken of the individual's search for self-knowledge and self-realization. But it is interesting to note that in the modern world the same questions are asked both individually and collectively. Not just "Who am I?" but also, "Who are we? Where are our roots? Where are we going?" Indeed, a whole array of sciences are reflecting on ourselves, our place in the universe, our relationship to space-time, our common origin and our common destiny. Just as there comes a period in the human life cycle when men and women pause to take stock of themselves as individuals, looking back and looking forward, so the human race now seems to be at a point in its history when it asks about its collective origin, its collective destiny and its collective identity.

And just as individuals can be authentic or inauthentic, so also can groups and even civilizations. Just as individuals can make progress or decline, can realize themselves or destroy themselves, so also can whole cultures be attentive or inattentive, intelligent or stupid, reasonable or unreasonable, responsible or irresponsible, loving or hate-filled. Whole cultures can transcend themselves and aspire to greatness while the same cultures, locked up in themselves, can wither and die. This is indeed a sobering thought in our turbulent twentieth century.

And as the individual only realizes himself or herself through death, so, the Christian story tells us, the human race will only reach self-realization at the omega point in the fullness of time. Only then will it cry out with one voice: "Abba! Father!"

In Buddhism

I

Self-realization lies at the very heart of Buddhism. Indeed, the great Buddhist religion began when Shakyamuni sat beneath the bodhi tree at Benares and attained the wonderful enlightenment that liberated him from the shackles of space and time. On the occasion of this awakening, which was also a self-realization, the enlightened one enunciated the four noble truths and the eightfold path. This latter speaks of eight ways to enlightenment, which are:

> Right understanding
> Right thought
> Right speech
> Right action
> Right livelihood
> Right effort
> Right mindfulness
> Right concentration

Since that time, Buddhists of all sects have imitated the Buddha in striving to walk these paths, and this has been their way to authenticity, to self-realization, to enlightenment.

But it should be noted that Buddhists, like Christians, do not strive for self-realization in a vacuum. They have their liturgy, their ritual, their sutras, their myths and, above all, a total commitment to the Buddha, the *dharma* and the *sangha*. And it should further be noted that this commitment to the Buddha is not a commitment to the historical Shakyamuni like the commitment Christians make to Jesus of Nazareth. *By the Buddha is meant the true self*, which, it is believed, is awakened in Buddhists just as it was awakened in the founder, Shakyamuni, in the fifth century B.C.

II

Let me now mention very briefly some Buddhist ways to self-realization.

In Pure Land Buddhism the believer finds enlightenment by reciting the name of Amida with faith. This enlightenment, however, is not a sudden illumination that can be obtained in this life. Rather does it consist in liberation from bad *karma* and rebirth in the Pure Land at the moment of death, for Amida has vowed that all who call upon his name with faith will be saved. And so the name of Amida is constantly on the lips of the believer: *Namu Amida Butsu*. (Honor and glory to the Buddha Amida).

In other forms of Buddhism the true self is found through mindfulness. One just sits and becomes aware of one's breathing and one's body as well as of the surroundings—of the wind and the rain and the waterfall. Distractions and fears and anxieties may float across the mind, but one simply lets them come and lets them go, always asking the question: "Who is listening? Who is the master who is listening?" and in this simple way the true self shines forth with great joy, and a tremendous liberation from anxiety is effected.

Again, one may attain to realization through meditation on the koan. About the koan I will speak in detail later. Here let me say that the *koan* is a zen story or problem that is constantly kept before the mind's eye until one breaks through to enlightenment and to realization of one's true self. The first and most important koan in the famous collection known as the *Mumonkan* runs as follows:

> A monk once asked Master Joshu, "Has a dog the Buddha nature?"
> Joshu answered, "Mu."

And the process by which one solves the koan and becomes one's true self is vividly described by Mumon:

> Arouse your entire body with its three hundred and sixty bones and joints and its eighty-four thousand pores of the skin; summon up a spirit of great doubt and concentrate on this word "Mu." Carry it continuously day and night. Do not form a nihilistic conception of vacancy, or a relative conception of "has" or "has not." It will be just as if you swallowed a red-hot iron ball, which you cannot spit out even if you try. All the illusory ideas and delusive thoughts accumulated up to the present will be exterminated, and when the time comes, internal and external will be spontaneously united. You will know this, but for yourself only, like a dumb man who has had a dream. Then all of a sudden an explosive conversion will occur, and you will astonish the heaven and shake the earth.[4]

Mumon goes on to say that if you meet the Buddha you will kill him, if you meet the patriarchs you will kill them. You will be overwhelmed with triumphant joy.

In all this, one finds one's true self by identifying with *mu*, by becoming *mu*. And while *mu* is a negative word, translated as *nothing*, it is clear that the experience itself is radiantly positive and joyful and powerful. It is indeed a triumphant discovery of one's true self, but it must be translated into the daily process of living and integrated into all that one does.

This true self is described in glowing terms by those who have attained to enlightenment. One of these, the Zen Master Shibayama, speaks of it as "absolute subjectivity," free from the limitations of space and time, life and death, subject and object, and "although it lives in an individual it is not restricted to the individual."[5] He then continues:

> Master Gudo calls this Absolute Subjectivity "the youth of natural beauty" which is genuine beauty undefiled by any artificiality. Referring to Seishi and Yoki, who are noted as the most beautiful women in the history of China, Gudo illustrates the absoluteness of the youth's natural

beauty by saying that even such rare beauties would look faded beside it.[6]

I myself heard Master Zenkei Shibayama speak about his own experience of enlightenment and I recall the joy and enthusiasm with which he talked about the youth of natural beauty. He himself, though very old, seemed to possess a certain youth that had nothing to do with chronological time. Rather than youth one might call it timelessness. It was very attractive and, no doubt, it stemmed from his discovery of his true self, the youth of natural beauty.

In this book, however, I make no claim to speak with authority about self-realization in Buddhism (that must be left to Buddhists); my intention is to write about Christian spirituality in dialogue with Buddhism. I want to ask what Christians who strive for self-realization in accordance with their own faith can learn from Buddhist practice. Such a question can now be asked in view of the fact that some zen masters speak freely about the Bible while Christians are gradually learning from Buddhists new things about their own spiritual path.[7]

III

Some zen masters, referring to the text, "Truly, I say to you, unless you turn and become like little children, you will never enter the kingdom of heaven" (Matt. 18:3), compare the mind of a child to the *mirror mind* about which zen constantly speaks. One of the aims of zen is to come to possess the mirror mind. Just as the pure and polished mirror is completely transparent, receiving everything into itself without distortion and reflecting all objects as if they were appearing in it for the first time, so the enlightened mind is completely receptive and filled with wonder, seeing everything as if for the first time.

This mirror mind is also called no-mind (because it is totally open and never fixed on one thing) and one attains to this no-mind by the mindfulness I have already described or by becoming *mu* or by identifying with other *koans* in the great collections. Zen masters, then, will say that the mirror mind is *mu* and the mind of the child is *mu*.

This is surely a great insight for a Christian who wants to grasp the message underlying the words of Jesus. Too often we Christians want simply to understand the words of Jesus intellectually without making them part of our lives. Here is a way by which one can come to *live* the gospel; one can become *mu*, become the mirror, become the child.

Only I would add to this zen interpretation a dimension that is peculiarly Christian. When Jesus uses this image he undoubtedly thinks not only of the unsullied, receptive and open mind of the child but also of the child *in relationship to its father*. When the child asks for bread, the father does not give it a stone but pours into the child's mind and heart an abundance of love and compassion. And so in this context the child—yes, possesses the mirror mind but a mirror mind that is totally open to receive love. When I become the child I realize existentially in the depths of my being that God my Father is love and that we did not first love him but that he first loved us. And having realized this I cry out: "Abba, Father!"

It is truly an extraordinary thing to become a child of God. It is truly an extraordinary thing to be a mirror that is totally open to receive love. For in this way I become an image of the Father (just as Jesus was an image of the Father) and in this way I realize my true self. This is the self-realization that can be expressed in the words of John: "See what love the Father has given us, that we should be called children of God; and so we are" (1 John 3:1).

IV

Closely allied to the notion of the mirror is that of one's original face. Zen frequently speaks of one's original face before one's parents were born, asserting that to discover one's original face is to be enlightened. This way of speaking may sound strange, even absurd, to Western ears, but it is a way of thinking that is deeply engrained in oriental thought, going back to primitive yoga where we find a form of meditation in which one travels back in time to early childhood, to the moment of birth, to the moment of conception, to past lives and on to the origin of all things.

And the notion of an existence before one's parents were born is not completely absent from the Hebrew tradition. Listen to the powerful words addressed to Jeremiah on the occasion of his prophetic call:

> Before I formed you in the womb I knew you,
> and before you were born I consecrated you;
> I appointed you a prophet to the nations. [Jer. 1:5]

On hearing these words spoken in the depths of his being, Jeremiah experiences his true self as it existed from eternity in the mind of God. This is the self that is spaceless and timeless like the youth of natural beauty; and yet it is (and here is the specifically Hebrew dimension) a self that is uniquely loved and chosen.

Again, the Bible frequently speaks of the name, whether it be the name of people or the name of God, and we know that the Hebrews used "name" in contexts where modern languages would speak of "person" or "self." In calling Abraham or Samuel by name, Yahweh is awakening in them the true self. When Jesus called Magdalen by name she, too, realized the deep self that had been slumbering until that moment. "Jesus said to her, 'Mary.' She turned and said to him, 'Rabboni' (which means Teacher)" (John 20:16). And many Christian contemplatives speak of a similar experience; they have heard their name called in the depth of their being and in that moment have realized themselves as truly and uniquely loved. Nor is this the name given them by their parents. It is that other name that existed before they were born and before they were in the womb, the name that expresses their true essence because it existed from eternity in the mind of God.

Note that Magdalen *turned;* and note that in the other text Jesus says: "Truly, I say to you, unless you *turn* . . ." (Matt. 18:3). This turning is a *metanoia* which closely resembles the zen *satori* or enlightenment. Only through a profound enlightenment could Magdalen recognize Jesus and find herself as uniquely loved. Only through such a turning can one truly become the child or *mu* or the mirror. And only through a profound enlightenment can one existentially understand these texts of the Bible.

But let me return to the original face. The Bible speaks frequently about the face of God which Moses longed to see but could not: "But," he said, "you cannot see my face; for man shall not see me and live" (Exod. 33:20). Like Moses we all wish to see the face of God and we can sing with the psalmist: "When shall I come and behold the face of God." (Ps. 42:2) And Paul finds this glory of God in the face of Jesus Christ, a face which is radiant like the face of Moses when he came down from the mountain. And here is where we see the original face, the face of God—we see it in Jesus and in the members of Jesus and in ourselves. This is indeed a great enlightenment. Sometimes we hear people say that they see the face of Jesus in a friend or that the friend sees the face of Jesus in them. Is this just pious talk? I do not think so. I believe it is a real enlightenment and one that is at the very heart of Christian *agape*—one that is the ideal of Christian friendship.

V

I have pointed to Christian experiences that may be understood more profoundly in the light of Buddhist practice. But I do not wish to make the unforgivable error of claiming that Buddhists and Christians are "saying the same thing," for the differences are obvious. The chief difference, it seems to me, is that in the Hebrew-Christian tradition *the true self is essentially relational*. I find my true self by going beyond this true self to the other. If my true self is a mirror, this mirror reflects a face other than my own—yet this other face becomes mine in a remarkable way. For what union could be closer than that of the pure mirror and the object it reflects? In self-realization I become one with God just as the object is one with the mirror and just as Jesus is one with his Father. And yet (paradox of paradoxes) I can cry out to the God with whom I am one; I can cry out, as Jesus cried out, "Abba, Father!"

VI

I have spoken of the true self as the youth of natural beauty, as the mirror mind, as the original face; and such beautiful symbols could be multiplied. But here let me pause to recall that both Buddhism and Christianity are profoundly realistic; both are well aware that the beauty of self is only part of the picture. In the Buddhist meditation called "mindfulness" one is encouraged to reflect not only on one's breathing and the beautiful surroundings but also on the ugliness that is within oneself.

And again, monks, a monk reflects precisely on this body itself, encased in skin and full of various impurities, from the soles of the feet upward and from the crown of the head downward, that: There is connected with this body hair of the head, hair of the body, nails, teeth, skin, flesh, sinews, bones, marrow, kidneys, heart, liver, membranes, spleen, lungs, intestines, mesentery, stomach, excrement, bile, phlegm, pus, blood, sweat, fat, tears, serum, saliva, mucus, synovic fluid, urine. . . . And again, monks, a monk might see a body in various stages of decomposition in a cemetery."[8]

And the same monks are asked to contemplate the vice and crime, the hatred and confusion that can exist in the human mind.

And all this is brought out somewhat shockingly in a *koan* that runs as follows:

A monk asked Unmon, "What is the Buddha?" Unmon replied, "A dried shit-stick."[9]

A shit-stick was used in China instead of toilet paper. And Unmon, asked about the wonderful Buddha nature that is the true self, makes this shocking and iconoclastic answer. What does he mean?

He means that however noble our aspirations, we must remember that we are (in the words of one commentator) "a bag of manure." Nor is it sufficient to give an intellectual assent to this proposition. One who would solve the *koan* must live it, realize it, act it out with his or her body, demonstrate to the master that one has identified with this ugly shit-stick.

And so we come up against the great paradox of human nature: We are at the same time saints and sinners, angels and demons, beautiful and ugly, the youth of natural beauty and the dried shit-stick. This way of thinking is found in St. Paul who can cry: "When I am weak, then I am strong" (2 Cor. 12:10). This is the Paul who reminds us that we carry a beautiful treasure in earthen vessels (2 Cor. 4:7). This is the Paul who knows that he is deeply wounded; that there is always a thorn in the flesh, a messenger of Satan to harass him; and that, however great the visions and revelations and enlightenments, this wound will never be totally healed until he sees the face of God.

But Paul glories in his weakness. The thought of his infirmity fills him with joy; he is triumphant. And the Buddhist realization that one is a dried shit-stick is also accompanied by great joy. There is no gnawing guilt in this *koan* but a great emancipation from anxiety together with the overflowing joy that always accompanies recognition of truth.

In the Christian Tradition

I

I have spoken about self-realization in modern thought and in a Christianity that dialogues with Buddhism. Now let me look at the specifically Christian tradition.

St. Teresa of Avila (1515–1582) in her inimitable, homely way speaks to her sisters about the necessity of self-knowledge:

> It is no small pity, and should cause us no little shame, that, through our own fault, we do not understand ourselves, or know who we are. Would it not be a sign of great ignorance, my daughters, if a person were asked who he was and could not say, and had no idea who his father or his mother was, or from what country he came?[10]

Anyone who has read Teresa knows that she has profound knowledge of her own interior castle and has seen the youth of natural beauty. She writes enthusiastically that she thinks of the soul "as if it were a castle made of a single diamond or a very clear crystal, in which there are many rooms, just as in Heaven there are many mansions . . . the soul of the righteous man is nothing but a paradise, in which, as God tells us, He takes His delight."[11]

Teresa, however, is acutely aware that this beauty is not, so to speak, inherent in the psyche but is derived from the Master who dwells within and is a reflection of his beauty; she is very eloquent in describing the "hideousness" of a soul from which God is absent:

> . . . I want you to consider what will be the state of this castle, so beautiful and resplendent, this Orient pearl, this tree of life . . . when the soul falls into mortal sin. No thicker darkness exists, and there is nothing dark and black which is not much less so than this."[12]

In all this, Teresa is writing out of her own experience (for she is no speculative theologian); but she also sings in harmony with the great chorus of Christian mystics from Gregory of Nyssa to Augustine and on to St. John of the Cross. Yes, the soul is beautiful, exquisitely beautiful, because it is made in the image of God; but separated from God, it is nothing. I am good and beautiful precisely because I am a mirror that reflects the goodness and beauty of Christ. And Christ, in turn, is a mirror that reflects the goodness and beauty of the Father. For "he is the image of the invisible God, the first born of all creatures" (Col. 1:15).

All this is in the mind of St. John of the Cross when, towards the end of his great poem *The Spiritual Canticle* he has the bride cry out ecstatically to the bridegroom:

> Let us rejoice, beloved,
> And let us go forth
> To behold ourselves in your beauty[13]

The image, of course, is that of the mirror. The soul, looking into the mirror which is the Risen Jesus, sees his beauty and, at the same time, sees her own beauty. Both are united in an extraordinary experience of joy. And in his commentary St. John of the Cross, identifying with the bride, looks to the bridegroom who is Christ and exclaims:

> . . . that I may resemble you in your beauty and you resemble me in your beauty, and my beauty may be your beauty and your beauty my beauty; wherefore I shall be you in your beauty, and you will be me in your beauty, because your beauty will be my beauty; and therefore we shall behold each other in your beauty".[14]

Your beauty will be my beauty! What a remarkable use of the mirror image! And does it not bring out the real friendship and equality between the human person and the Risen Jesus whom he or she loves? Does it not bring out powerfully the "divinization" of the human person through the Risen Jesus? Here we are at the peak point of Christian mystical self-realization.

II

St. John of the Cross is part of a tradition, but rather than go deeply into this tradition that gave him birth, let me go back to his ultimate source—the New Testament. Here the questions, "Who are you?" and "What is your name?" keep recurring. Just as Moses asked Yahweh who he was, so the priests and levites came to John and asked: " 'Who are you?' He confessed, he did not deny, but confessed, 'I am not the Christ' and they asked him, 'What then? Are you Elijah?' He said, 'I am not.' 'Are you the prophet?' And he answered, 'No.' They said to him then, 'Who are you? Let us have an answer for those who sent us. What do you say about yourself?' " (John 1:19–22).

There is a note of urgency, almost of frustration, in their questions. John answers:

> I am the voice of one crying in the wilderness, "Make straight the way of the Lord," as the prophet Isaiah said. [John 1:23]

John's whole identity consists in being the precursor; he defines himself in *his relationship to Jesus*. Later, in the same gospel, he poetically calls himself "the friend of the bridegroom" (John 3:29). And cannot every Christian say the same? Does not every Christian define himself or herself in relationship to Jesus? Are we not all friends of the bridegroom—and through the friendship, children of the Father?

And this is pre-eminently true of Paul, whose life can be seen as a search for the true self, the true Paul who begins to emerge at that meeting with Jesus on the road to Damascus. "And he said, 'Who are you, Lord?' " (Acts 9:5). In finding Jesus, Paul finds himself, or begins to find himself; he sets out on a journey of self-realization that extends over the whole cycle of his life.

And Paul's quest is filled with anguishing struggle. He does not understand himself, for he does not what he wants but does the very thing he hates and he laments: " . . . it is no longer I that do it, but sin which dwells within me" (Rom. 7:20). Paul finds two selves: one is his "inmost self," and the other is in his members:

> For I delight in the law of God in my
> inmost self, but I see in my members another
> law at war with the law of my mind . . . [Rom. 7:22–23]

And so the struggle of Paul's life is to find the inmost self, to act from the inmost self, and to be liberated from the law of evil. "Who will deliver me from the body of death?" he cries and he answers his own question: "Thanks be to God through Jesus Christ our Lord!" (Rom. 7:24–25).

And so Paul finds his identity and describes himself in clear-cut terms: "Paul, a servant of Jesus Christ, called to be an apostle, set apart for the gospel of God . . ." (Rom. 1:1). And his intimacy with Jesus is always growing, so that he can say that he counts everything as loss because of the surpassing worth of knowing and loving Christ Jesus his Lord. And his ideal is clear: " . . . that I may know him and the power of his resurrection, and may share his sufferings, becoming like him in his death, that if possible I may attain the resurrection from the dead" (Phil. 3:10, 11). Paul is running after Jesus like an athlete in the Isthmyan games, but eventually he dies to himself to live to Jesus. For Jesus is not outside but is dwelling within, and Paul can cry: "I have been crucified with Christ; it is no longer I who live, but Christ who lives in me . . ." (Gal. 2:20). Yet Paul's journey does not stop with his union with Jesus; it goes on to the Father of Our Lord Jesus Christ. Since through Jesus he is a son, he can call God his Father. The same holds true for us and Paul tells us:

> And because you are sons, God has
> sent the Spirit of his Son into
> our hearts crying, "Abba, Father!" [Gal. 4:6]

And so Paul finds his true self in a Trinitarian experience. United with Jesus and filled with the Spirit he cries out: "Abba, Father!" And we, too, aided by grace will find enlightenment in this way.

III

I have spoken about the identity of the Johannine John the Baptist and of Paul. Is it possible to speak also about the self-realization of Jesus? I have already said that Buddhism is founded upon the self-realization of Shakyamuni the Buddha. Can we say that Christianity is founded upon the self-realization of Jesus?

I believe that this question can be answered in the affirmative. I believe that Christianity is founded on the mystical experience of Jesus and, above all, upon his experience of who he was. I believe that the basis of Christianity is the experience Jesus had of his relationship with his Father—a relationship to which those who believe in him can aspire. But granted all this, anyone who embarks on a study of Jesus the mystic is up against a formidable problem of methodology.

For modern exegetes agree that a critical biography of Jesus cannot be written. We just do not have the evidence. The gospels, composed many decades after the death of Jesus, were written in the light of the resurrection and contain much theological reflection as well as interpretations that are the fruit of the religious experience of the early Christian community. And this means that the "Jesus of history," as a critical biographer might understand this phrase, is veiled from our eyes.

Yet I believe it is theologically legitimate and not unscholarly to take the gospels as they stand, believing that they were written under the guidance of the Spirit and that they are *true interpretations* of the life and deeds of Jesus. I believe that by prayerful reflection on the gospel narratives one can come to a knowledge of the heart of Jesus— the risen and the earthly Jesus. This has been the practice of Christians for almost two thousand years, and I cannot believe that these Christians have been deceived.[15]

Such is the approach of Karl Rahner when, in an important article entitled "Dogmatic Reflections on the Knowledge and Self-Consciousness of Christ," he argues that Jesus, being truly man, had an authentically human experience, and that part of this experience was his gradual discovery of his true self.[16] To understand this way of thinking it is necessary to recall once more the distinction between *knowing* a thing and *being conscious* of it. From the dawn of consciousness, Jesus was *conscious* in the depth of his being of his divinity, but only through growth and development did he come to understand, objectify and really *know* what was previously hidden. And in this way he had a truly human experience while being divine. Luke tells us that Jesus "increased in wisdom and in stature and in favor with God and man" (Luke 2:52). And can we not say that he grew to self-realization through the process of living with all its joy and pain, through divine inspirations during the day and during those long nights of prayer, through his conflict with the tempter, through his constant reading of the Hebrew scriptures wherein he saw himself mirrored? And can we not say that his discovery of self was completed through his death and resurrection, when he was, in the words of Paul "designated Son of God in power according to the Spirit of holiness in his resurrection from the dead" (Rom. 1:4)? To find his glorified self Jesus had to suffer. "Was it not necessary that the Christ should suffer these things and enter into his glory?" (Luke 24:26).

But it is principally in the fourth gospel, every page of which is influenced by faith in the resurrection, that we find a Jesus who is acutely aware of his identity: He is aware that he is only son of the Father; he is aware that he comes from God and returns to God; he is aware that he is from above. This is the Jesus who can say confidently: "I know whence I have come and whither I am going . . ." (John 8:14). This is the Jesus on whose lips the evangelist puts those words of Exodus: I am: ἐγὼ ἐμί. When we hear Jesus say, "Before Abraham was I am . . ." (John 8:58); or when we hear him utter those great "I am's"—I am the door, the bread, the light, the way, the truth, the resurrection—when we hear all this, we are brought back to the name of Yahweh: "I AM WHO I AM . . . Say this to the people of Israel, 'I AM has sent me to you' " (Exod. 3:14).

And so the deep self of Jesus is outside space and time, since he is the eternal word of the Father. And Jesus can finally say: "He who has seen me has seen the Father" (John 14:9). For he is the perfect image of the Father, the mirror in which the Father is reflected.

Here we are at the very heart of Johannine theology. Jesus understands and knows himself *in relationship to his Father*. Indeed his whole being is relational and oriented to the Father, just as the Father is relational and oriented to the Son. One cannot but recall that passage in Matthew which is profoundly Johannine in flavor: "All things have been delivered to me by my Father; and no one knows the Son except the Father, and no one knows the Father except the Son and anyone to whom the Son chooses to reveal him" (Matt. 11:27).

But if we want to understand the self-realization of Jesus as depicted in the gospels, we must carry our search one step further and ask about his relationship with the human race. And here C. H. Dodd, commenting on the fourth gospel and stressing the real humanity of Jesus, writes:

> And yet, says the Evangelist, in all this He was much more than one individual among many, *He was the true self of the human race*, standing in

that perfect union with God to which others can attain only as they are incorporate in him . . .[17]

Jesus was the true self of the human race. What remarkable implications for the mystical life can be found in this statement! Already this idea is adumbrated in the synoptic gospels where Jesus identifies with the hungry, the thirsty, the naked and those in prison—"as you did it to one of the least of these my brethren, you did it to me" (Matt. 25:40). One recalls how Paul speaks of "the one man Jesus Christ," thanks to whom grace abounds for many (Rom. 5:15). One recalls that the Second Vatican Council claimed that Christ reveals man to himself, as if to say that Christ is the great mirror in which humanity stands reflected.

And all of this is of the greatest practical importance for Christians who would search for their true self; because one central point of the New Testament is that those who believe in Jesus can have with the Father the same relationship that Jesus had. As he called "Abba, Father," we also can call "Abba, Father!" As he identified with the sick and afflicted, we also can identify with the sick and afflicted. As he died and rose, we die and rise. As he was divine by nature, we are divine by grace. His self-realization is our self-realization. For he is the archetypal man.

IV

Let me end this chapter, as I began, with modern men and women entering into the depths of their own consciousness in search of themselves. What a journey! And as we pass through the outer layers of turbulent darkness and approach the core of our being, what will we find? Will we find a mirror? And if so, what face will be relected in that mirror? Will it be the face of one who was pronounced dead? Will we discover that God, who seemed to die in the outer world, has dramatically come to life in the inner world of consciousness? I think we will. If we have the courage to answer the call to look into the mirror of our own souls, we will see our own beauty and the beauty of God. And that will be a great enlightenment.

NOTES

1. Here let me distinguish between self-realization and self-actualization. This latter, in my terminology, is a horizontal process by which I come to actuate and use all my human potential. About this I do not speak. Self-realization is a vertical movement by which, plunging to the depth of my being, I discover my true self and become my true self.
2. Bernard Lonergan, *A Second Collection* (Philadelphia: Westminster Press; London: Darton, Longman and Todd, 1974), p. 269.
3. *Spiritual Exercises of St. Ignatius,* Rules for Discernment of Spirits, No. 5.
4. Katsuki Sekida, trans., *Two Zen Classics: Mumonkan and Hekiganroku* (New York and Tokyo: Weatherhill, 1977), p. 28.
5. Zenkei Shibayama, *Zen Comments on the Mumonkan* (New York: Harper & Row, 1974), p. 96.
6. Ibid.
7. See especially the excellent book by Kakichi Kadowaki, *Zen and the Bible* (London: Routledge and Kegan Paul, 1979).
8. Edward Conze, ed., *Buddhist Texts* (New York: Harper & Row, 1964).
9. *Mumonkan,* Case 21.
10. St. Teresa of Avila, *Interior Castle,* trans. Allison Peers (New York: Doubleday Image Books, 1961), chap. 1.
11. Ibid.
12. Ibid., chap. 2.
13. *Spiritual Canticle,* st. 36.
14. Ibid., st. 36, no. 5.
15. Scripture scholars are moving away from the naive realism that would say that some witnesses saw the *facts* and others later wrote an *interpretation,* and that, in consequence, we can believe the first set of witnesses and must be wary of the so-called interpreters. Peter Chirico puts it well: "With regard to Christ . . . every account of his activity, whether true or false, is an interpretation. The fathers, the councils, and the scholastic theologians have given us only interpretations. Moreover, even the New Testament writers and before them the original witnesses possessed, and were able to pass on, not the concrete reality of Christ but only their limited interpretations. All these views are necessarily interpretations, because the intelligibility of concrete reality is so vast and the possibilities of any human intellect so limited that a total uninterpreted grasp of any reality is impossible." Chirico goes on to say that the interpretation of the eye-witnesses is not necessarily more valuable than that of the later writers. See Peter Chirico, "Hans Küng's Christology: An Evaluation of Its Presuppositions," *Theological Studies,* June 1979.
16. Karl Rahner, *Theological Investigations,* Vol. 5 (New York: Seabury; London: Darton, Longman and Todd, 1966), pp. 193 ff. Rahner observes that "knowledge has a multi-layered structure: this means that it is absolutely possible that in relation to these different dimensions of consciousness and knowledge something may be known and not known at the same time."
17. C. H. Dodd, *The Interpretation of the Fourth Gospel* (Cambridge, Eng.: Cambridge University Press, 1970).

3

Body and Breathing

E ASTERN MEDITATION FROM yoga to zen attaches the greatest importance to the body and the breathing. The Buddhist or the Hindu does not reach enlightenment through some purely spiritual activity of the mind but through a long and rigorous training in breathing, in posture and in diet. This is a training not of the mind alone nor of the body alone but of the body-person, of the mind-and-body.

And the bodily dimension should also be of primary importance in the Christian way—a way that, far from annihilating the body and the senses, aims at transforming them. While it is true that certain currents of Christian spirituality were influenced by (might I say "contaminated" by?) a neoplatonic rejection of matter, let us never forget that authentic Christianity follows one who saw a sacramental dimension in the human body, in the flowers of the field and in the whole material world. "Is not . . . the body more than clothing?" he asked (Matt. 6:25), as if to say that the body is the primary gift of our heavenly Father. "Consider the lilies . . ." he said (Matt. 6:28), as he reflected on the care of our heavenly Father for nature. And at the Last Supper he uttered those shattering words that we call the mystery of faith: "This is my body" (Matt. 26:26).

And yet, in spite of all this, many modern Christians feel that the bodily dimension of their prayer and worship has been sadly neglected and is woefully underdeveloped. And they realize that dialogue with the great religions of the East can be powerfully fruitful precisely in this area. Some would go further and say that Christianity *needs* oriental insights if it is to teach a meditation that is healthy and whole.

Let me, then, consider this matter in a practical way, and let me begin with the breathing.

The Way of the Breath

I

It would be an exaggeration to say that training of the breath is an essential part of the spiritual journey. For some people attending to the breath is a distraction rather than a help, and such people would do best to forget it. But, having said this, it is also true that for other people, both Christian and Buddhist, the whole spiritual path is a matter of breathing. They walk "the way of the breath" and have little need for words. Furthermore, it can be said that throughout East Asia, training of the breath is considered a natural first step in the spiritual path. To meditate without learning to breathe would be like eating without learning to use chopsticks. One might succeed, but in a very clumsy way.

Let me, then, say a brief word about correct breathing, selecting three points from Dr. Tomio Hirai, who, being a physician, writes not of those esoteric forms of breathing that can be dangerous to physical and psychological health but of a simple method that is completely safe and beneficial for mind and body.[1]

First of all, correct breathing is slow. And to make it slow one simply lengthens the exhalation—gives out long, slow, gentle breaths, always breathing through the nose. One should never strain or do violence to oneself and, indeed, if one simply observes or "follows" the breath, it will naturally become slower with little or no effort. The ordinary person breathes from sixteen to eighteen times a minute but if one "follows" the breath it will quickly slow down to ten and even to five or six times a minute.

Second, correct breathing is rhythmical. Ordinarily our breathing is irregular, dominated by our emotional life and our changes of mood, but one can, again, regulate the breathing by being aware of it, or following it, in an effortless way. In his excellent little book *Zen Mind, Beginners Mind* Shunryu Suzuki tells us that if we want to control people we should neither interfere with them nor neglect them. We should simply *watch* them. And the same holds true for the breath. If we want to control it, to make it slow and rhythmical, it is sufficient to watch it and soon we will find that it is under our control.[2]

Third, correct breathing is abdominal. As one breathes in, one swells the muscles of the lower abdomen and becomes aware of the *tanden*, the point about one inch below the navel which, in traditional Sino-Japanese thought, is the body's center of gravity. One soon experiences great strength in the lower belly.

These three points are made by Dr. Hirai. But if one would master the art of breathing it is not sufficient to read books; there is no substitute for practice. One must *do* it. Whether sitting still in the cross-legged position or sitting on a bus or a train, one can first discover one's breath, be aware of the fact that one is breathing and then count the exhalations; or one can follow the breath, repeating to oneself: "I will breathe in; I will breathe out." This should be done in a gentle and effortless way, without force of any kind.

And if one practices constantly, one's own method develops from within. For there is a personal dimension to all this, and one must finally discover one's own way. There is a zen saying that "even Buddhas do but point the way," meaning that in the last analysis no one can teach you the way: You must find it for yourself.

II

And the discovery of one's personal way of breathing is in itself a small enlightenment. Like Archimedes one exclaims: "Eureka!" "I have it; let no one tell me otherwise!" Now there comes great peace and joy in attentiveness to this slow, rhythmical breathing, and one loves to return to the breath at various times during the day. In this context, Anthony de Mello quotes an oriental master who would say to his disciples: "Your breathing is your greatest friend. Return to it in all your troubles and you will find comfort and guidance."[3] How true! Return to the breath gives strength and helps us discern our way.

The joy of breathing stems partly from the physical benefits. In deep, abdominal breathing, the body is purified. Exhalation removes the carbon dioxide in the lungs, while inhalation carries to the body a fresh supply of oxygen; moreover, experts tell us that slow, deep breathing lightens the load the heart must bear. But even more important are the emotional and psychological benefits. Through breathing one gets in touch with one's belly, with one's *viscera*, with one's feelings, with one's life. What a glorious thing for poor modern men and women who are split, divided, torn asunder! They will find harmony by reflecting on the words of Jesus: "Is not life more than food and the body more than clothing?" (Matt. 6:25). For one who walks the way of the breathing experiences life, experiences the body, and knows existentially that the words of Jesus are true.

And, as one breathes, inner unification grows. Zen speaks of breathing through every pore and this is literally true. One gradually becomes aware that the whole body is breathing and that the whole body is meditating. "The breathing in zazen practice controls the pores of the skin, the circulation of the blood, and even the activity of the capillary vessels. Zen breathing and posture control skin sensation, which in turn controls the peace of both heart and mind. The quietness of absolute samadhi comes from pacified skin sensation."[4]

One may now become aware of the cosmic dimension of the body, of one's union with the whole universe and of "the breathing of the universe." Shunryu Suzuki states it well:

> When we practice zazen our mind always follows our breathing. When we inhale, the air comes into the inner world. When we exhale, the air goes out to the outer world. The inner world is limitless, and the outer world is also limitless. We say "inner world" or "outer world," but actually this is just one whole world. In this limitless world, our throat is like a swinging door. The air comes in and goes out like someone passing through a swinging door.[5]

From all this it will be clear that there is a whole spirituality of the breath, or, as I have said, a "way of the breath." It is a truly great way to self-realization.

But at this point someone may say: "And what has all this to do with religion? How can it lead to God?"

True enough, the type of breathing I have described is taught to those who practice *karate* and *judo* and the tea ceremony and flower arrangement. Such people frequently meditate before beginning their sport or their art. And in the modern world the art of breathing is taught to singers, to joggers, to mothers in childbirth, and to a host of people who find that correct breathing helps their work or profession. So where does religion fit in?

And here I would make an important distinction between *breathing for the development of human potential* and *breathing with faith*. It is precisely faith that makes breathing a religious exercise and by faith I here mean total commitment to some ultimate reality. The zen master can, and does, distinguish between those who are sitting in meditation to develop their human powers and those who are practicing in order to find salvation through total commitment to the *dharma*. And one can again distinguish those who practice with total commitment through Jesus to the Father. But granted this, it is also true that the dividing line between secular meditation (if I may use the term) and religious meditation is often blurred. People may begin in order to develop human potential and discover that at some point, unknown to themselves, faith has begun to predominate.

III

And so breathing becomes an exercise of faith. Some people will breathe in silence without any words whatever; and in this silence they are present to the great mystery that dwells in them and in which they dwell. Other people prefer to use a word or phrase (it is sometimes said that a seven-syllable phrase is peculiarly suited to the normal rhythm of breathing) that they repeat again and again—until eventually it repeats itself. The orthodox tradition claims that when the Jesus prayer has entered into the rhythm of breath and has entered into the very body, one is at last obeying the words of the scripture that we should pray without ceasing. For now every breath, waking or sleeping, is an act of faith and an act of love.

If one continues on this path of faith one may come to the very apex of the mystical life and to the peak point of enlightenment. But it is also possible to be side-tracked and about this I will say a brief word.

Through breathing it is possible to cultivate all kinds of powers. It is claimed, for instance, that by breath control one can stay under water for half a day. This is innocent enough. But it is also claimed that the art of *ninjutsu*, or making oneself invisible, depends upon the breathing. Again, breathing is a way to mind expansion, to the opening of layers of consciousness that are normally dormant. Such use of the breath is found in yoga. "By making his respiration rhythmical and progressively slower," writes Eliade, "the yogin can 'penetrate'—that is, he can experience in perfect lucidity—certain states of consciousness that are peculiar to sleep."[6] Eliade then distinguishes four modalities of consciousness: the waking consciousness, consciousness in sleep with dreams, consciousness in dreamless sleep, and cataleptic consciousness or trance. "By means of *pranayama*—that is, by increasingly prolonging inhalation and exhalation (the goal of this practice being to allow as long an interval as possible to pass between the two moments of respiration)—the yogin can, then, penetrate all the modalities of consciousness."[7]

Through breathing also one can learn to control the heartbeat and the digestive functions. As I said in my book *Silent Music*, laboratory experiments are pointing to the extraordinary potential that is unleashed by breathing.

All this is of great scientific and human interest, but the great religious traditions agree that to aim at acquiring psychic powers, to become attached to them, to glory in them, to demonstrate them to others—that this is the temptation of temptations in the mystical path. It can lead to vanity and bring about one's downfall. At least it hinders spiritual progress. One must belittle these powers, for they are like the bewitchingly seductive sirens whose beautiful voices called out to Ulysses, begging him to come to their voluptuous embrace and to forget his journey homeward to the wise Penelope. Like Ulysses it may be necessary to have ourselves bound to the mast. If so, that is what we must do, for we must never get entangled with these fascinating creatures but let our ship speed onwards to our true home which is union with God.

But if we do avoid this attractive peril, if we pay no attention to extraordinary powers and never seek them, how does our journey continue?

IV

Here let me recall that the path of faith we have now entered is one of total renunciation. St. John of the Cross never tires of quoting the words of Jesus: "Whoever of you does not renounce all that he has cannot be my disciple" (Luke 14:33). And all means all. In consequence the time comes when one must leave the breath, forget the breath—transcend it, go beyond it into the night of faith and of nothingness. Not that we decide to enter this night or think that we can go into it by our own efforts. No, no. We only go if we are called. But if the call comes, we leave the breath. Just as we spurn the temptation to use it for extraordinary psychic feats so we spurn the temptation to relish its beauties and its joys. For the time for this is gone and what was previously a help may now be a hindrance. Now we are invited to go on a journey in which we must have neither gold nor silver nor copper in our belts. We must have no superfluous baggage, not even our own breathing.

I said that to enter the night we transcend the breathing, but this does not mean that we reject it. We go beyond without leaving it behind. We start to breathe in a completely new way. Let me endeavor to describe this by means of a comparison.

There is a zen koan which runs as follows:

Ho asked Basho: "What is it that transcends everything in the universe?"

Basho answered: "I will tell you after you have drunk up all the waters of the Western river in one gulp."

Ho said: "I have already drunk up all the waters of the Western river in one gulp."

Basho replied: "Then I have already answered your question."

Reflecting on this, one of my students composed a koan about the breathing:

Ho asked Basho: "What is the breathing of man which is not breathing?"

Basho replied: "I will tell you when you have breathed in the spirit of the universe in one breath."

Ho answered: "I have already breathed in the spirit of the universe in one breath."

Basho replied: "Then I have already answered your question."[8]

The breathing that is not breathing! The breathing that is one breath! How explain this outrageous paradox?

To understand this, one must recall that in the experience of the mystics there is not only a breathing that is not breathing, but also a seeing that is not seeing, a hearing that is not hearing, a smelling that is not smelling, a touching that is not touching, a tasting that is not tasting. In short, a whole gamut of *interior senses* opens up to one who enters the deeper mansions of the interior castle. Augustine of Hippo, who knew this well, speaks poetically and powerfully about these paradoxical interior senses that know God but do not know him. He is speaking about his knowledge of God and he first affirms dramatically that this knowledge is unlike anything his senses can attain to:

> What is it then that I love when I love you? Not bodily beauty, and not temporal glory, not the clear shining light, lovely as it is to our eyes, not the sweet melodies of many-moded songs, not the soft smell of flowers and ointments and perfumes, not manna and honey, not limbs made for the body's embrace, not these do I love when I love my God.

And so Augustine is quite clear that he loves nothing bodily and does not love in a bodily way. And yet he continues paradoxically to say that he *does* love in a sensible way, but with transfigured senses:

> Yet I do love a certain light, a certain voice, a certain odor, a certain food, a certain embrace when I love my God: a light, a voice, an odor, a food, an embrace for the man within me, where his light, which no place can contain, floods into my soul; where he utters words that time does not speed away; where he sends forth an aroma that no wind can scatter; where he provides food that no eating can lessen; where he so clings that satiety does not sunder us. This is what I love when I love my God.[9]

In this way Augustine speaks of a seeing that is not seeing, a hearing that is not hearing, a smelling that is not smelling, an embrace that is not embracing. And I might add (though Augustine does not refer to it) that there is a breathing that is not breathing.

This approach to God is systematized by Aquinas and the scholastics when they say that we can know God by affirmation, negation and pre-eminence. I affirm that God is beautiful; I deny that he is beautiful as we ordinarily experience beauty; I affirm that he is beautiful in a pre-eminent way. I affirm that God is light; I deny that he is light as we ordinarily experience light; I affirm that he is light in a pre-eminent way. And so for all the divine attributes. That is

why I can affirm that at the peak of the mystical life I breathe; I deny that it is breathing as I ordinarily experience breathing; I affirm that it is breathing in a pre-eminent way.

V

Now all this is of the greatest practical importance. Let me repeat: The authentic mystical path is not one of rejection but of transformation. The body is transformed; the seeing is transformed; the hearing is transformed; the smelling is transformed; the tasting is transformed; the breathing is transformed. This transformation is nothing other than the spiritualization of matter; and the process will continue until the final transformation takes place through death and resurrection. Moreover the dark night of the Christian mystical tradition is not a negative emptiness but a plenitude in which the senses and the intelligence are transformed. It all seems very dark, says St. John of the Cross, because our eyes are unaccustomed to it and cannot recognize the beauty. Only in time do we come to love the darkness and to realize that it is pre-eminently light.

And here I need hardly point out that this is in harmony with the New Testament, which speaks not of destruction but of a "new heaven and a new earth" (Rev. 21:1). It is in harmony with St. Paul, who speaks not of pure spirit but of a spiritualized body: "If there is a physical body, there is also a spiritual body" (1 Cor. 15:44). And Paul speaks of the great transformation that takes place through resurrection: "What is sown is perishable, what is raised is imperishable. It is sown in dishonor, it is raised in glory. It is sown in weakness, it is raised in power" (1 Cor. 15:43).

But let me return to the breathing.

At the apex of the mystical life, St. John of the Cross experiences the awakening of the word in the depths of his being and he cries out:

> And in Your sweet breathing
> Filled with good and glory,
> How tenderly You swell my heart with love.[10]

Of this breathing that is not breathing, the saint cannot speak. "I do not desire to speak of this breathing, filled for the soul with good and glory and delicate love of God, for I am aware of being incapable of so doing, and were I to try, it might seem less than it is."[11] And yet he tries to explain it—and he does so in a Trinitarian context, telling us that the ultimate breath to which all other breathing points is the Holy Spirit, who is the breath of God. At the apex of the mystical life, the Spirit breathes in me and, united with Jesus, I cry out: "Abba, Father!" It is now that the transformation is approaching completion, a completion that will only be reached when the veil of mortal life is torn away and I am face to face with God in the eternal mirror.

VI

I have spoken about the way of the breath practiced in the mysticism of all the great religions. If a Christian embarks on this journey it is very important that he or she should, like the disciples going to Emmaus, walk with Jesus. Practically this can be done by constant reading of the gospels or by using some form of the Jesus prayer with the breath—going beyond it when so called, and returning to it as to a base. Moreover, I have sometimes thought that as oriental Christianity develops we will see the rise of a devotion to the breath of Jesus. If we have devotion to the face of Jesus, to the wounds of Jesus, to the heart of Jesus, would not devotion to the breath of Jesus be profoundly meaningful? Then one would breathe the Holy Spirit in unison with Jesus. One would recall the Johannine Jesus who bowed his head and gave up his spirit, the Jesus who breathed on his apostles and said: "Receive the Holy Spirit . . ." (John 20:22). One would further recall the breath of God in Genesis and the great passage in Ezekiel where Yahweh breathes on the dry bones of Israel and gives them life. All this would help to develop the way of the breath within Christianity. And it would give a powerful impetus to Christian mysticism.

The Way of the Body

I

I have spoken about the breath, saying that in mystical experience one does not reject the breathing but goes beyond it to a "breathing that is not breathing." And I have further indicated that this principle applies not only to the breath but to all the senses and to the body itself. Mystical experience is nothing less than a transformation of the whole person in preparation for that final transformation that takes place through death and resurrection.

And having spoken about breathing I would now like to speak about the body, which is also of the greatest importance on the road to enlightenment and self-realization. To understand this one need only recall, with modern psychology, that the body talks. The face talks; the eyes talk; the throat talks; the limbs talk. If I enter a crowded room, my body is talking before I utter a single word, and one who has learned to read the body knows what I am saying. We all know that celebrities who appear on television talk not only with their lips but with their whole bodies; their lips utter what is in their conscious mind, but their bodies reveal the secrets of the unconscious.

And in meditation also the body talks. It talks to myself, it talks to others, and it talks to God. And oriental meditation has mastered this body language in an extraordinary way. This is particularly true of hatha yoga with its beautiful asanas of which the chief is the lotus posture, often called the *perfect posture*. And what does this perfect posture say? Buddhist tradition agrees that the lotus posture, properly assumed, reveals the true self, speaks of the true self. Not the little ego that is the subject of my desires but the self of the universe, eternal and serene. And ideally speaking (Buddhism will say) all our actions should reveal this true self; all our actions should spring from the center of the universe.

And so in all religions body language is used in prayer. The Hebrews often prayed by raising up their hands; and we find those terrible words of Yahweh in Isaiah:

> When you spread forth your hands,
> I will hide my eyes from you. [Isa. 1:15]

But in the Bible we find not only the raising of the hands but also the religious dance, made famous, indeed, by David who danced naked before the ark and earned the contempt of Michal, the daughter of Saul. And we see in the gospels a Jesus who was a master of body language: Jesus who washed the feet of the disciples; Jesus who wrote on the ground when they brought to him the woman taken in adultery; Jesus who said to the crowd: "I am"; and "they drew back and fell to the ground" (John 18:6). This is the Jesus who read the hearts of others, and I believe he could read hearts because he could read bodies.

II

In some forms of oriental meditation the first step is to become aware of one's body. One gets out of the head, so to speak, and returns to the senses; one becomes aware of every part of the body and feels the pulsation of life in one's whole being. And if one develops this awareness one quickly begins to realize that the body is very wise and tells us many things: when to eat and when to fast, when to sleep and when to watch, when to talk and when to be silent. Earlier in this book I spoke about listening to one's feelings, to one's process of thinking and to one's religious experience. Now let me add that this process of listening is not complete until one learns to listen also to the body.

In the Sino-Japanese tradition the most important part of the body, from which all power and energy flows, is the *tanden*, a point located about an inch below the navel. This *tanden* is represented by the characters:

丹

田

The first character, important in Chinese medicine, means red, or brightly colored or mercurial; it was associated with a medicine that, it was claimed, conferred immortality. The second character means field. And so the *tanden* is the field of mercurial power. It is also called *kikai*, which means "the sea of energy."

In the martial arts, as well as in zen, it is of the greatest importance to get in touch with one's *tanden*. One can do so through the breathing I described earlier in this chapter—*tanden breathing*. Or one can do so simply by polishing a table, using large circular movements but retaining the strength at the point below the navel.

Here let me say that while the West has frequently ridiculed oriental meditation as "navel gazing," the Sino-Japanese world has always maintained that this part of the body is extremely important, significant and symbolic. Through the navel one is in contact with one's mother, with one's prenatal life, with one's mother's mother, with one's original face, with the origin of all things. That is why it is not surprising that some zen masters should suggest quite literally that one contemplate one's navel from time to time. Nor is it surprising that just as the Western world waxes eloquent about the romantic role of the heart, so East Asia is equally eloquent about the dark power of the *hara* or belly. For just as the head stands for heaven or *yang*, so the belly stands for earth or *yin*. It also stands for the feminine and for the unconscious, which is the source of creativity and the spiritual womb of the human person—a womb that gives birth to great and liberating enlightenments, profound religious experience, artistic insights, epoch-making scientific discoveries.

Nor is this notion completely absent from the Hebrew tradition, where the *viscera* or guts are the seat of power and emotion. And does not Jesus say: "He who believes in me, as the scripture says, out of his belly (ἐκ τῆς κοιλίας) shall flow rivers of water" (John 7:38)? Here is indeed a powerful statement of the creativity of the *tanden*.

III

But as meditation develops, just as one transcends the breathing, so one transcends the *tanden*. Just as one must eventually forget the breathing, so one must eventually forget the body. But (and here we are back to the paradoxes) just as there is a breathing that is not breathing, so there is a center that is not a center. When I say that it is not a center, I mean that it is not located specifically at the navel or at any part of the body. But it is of the utmost importance, for it is nothing other than the true self. To this center we must return continually; we must never lose touch with it.

To illustrate this point there is in the *Mumonkan* a zen koan that runs as follows:

> Every day Master Zuigan Shigen would call out to himself, "Oh, Master" and would answer himself, "Yes" "Are you awake?" he would ask, and would answer, "Yes, I am." "Never be deceived by others, any day, any time" "No, I will not."[12]

Here the master to whom Zuigan calls is the center, the true self, the Buddha nature, the deepest part of his being. It is precisely here that one must always be awake; and if the true self is awake there can be no deceit because this true self, youth of natural beauty, always sees goodness and truth. And so one returns to the center. With Master Zuigan one can ask oneself the question in this koan. Or one can use another zen saying: "Examine the place where you stand." The meaning is that you should pause, recollect yourself, keep in touch with your deepest self.

The point I wish to make here, however, is that while this process of recollection is at first associated with the belly, one must go beyond the physical to a center that is spaceless and timeless. If one remains too long with the physical body, one's progress may be obstructed.

IV

The Christian mystical tradition has also set the highest store upon the center of the soul. This center is called the ground of being, the core of one's being, the divine spark, the *synteresis*, the *Seelenfünklein*. The author of *The Cloud* calls it "the sovereign point of the spirit" and in words that remind us of Master Zuigan he gives the good advice: "Hold yourself at the sovereign point of the spirit . . ." It is as if he were to say: "Keep in touch with your deepest self and with the core of your being."

In his *Return to the Center* Bede Griffiths argues convincingly that this center or core of the human person is precisely the point where Eastern and Western spirituality can meet, and he prefaces his book with a striking quotation from William Law (1688–1781):

> But there is a root or depth in thee from which all the faculties come forth, as lines from a center or as branches from the body of the tree. This depth is called the *Center*, the *Fund* or Bottom of the soul. This depth is the unity, the eternity, I had almost said the infinity of thy soul; for it is so infinite that nothing can satisfy it or give it rest but the infinity of God.[13]

This is well said. For the Christian mystical tradition claims that the center of the soul is precisely the point where man meets God and receives his being from God. Indeed, the scholastics raised the problem of how it was even possible for the created to meet the uncreated since there could be no meeting point between the finite and the infinite. And they answered their own question by speaking of a *potentia obedientialis*, meaning the capacity of the human to receive the divine. And of course this *potentia obedientialis* reached its total actuation in Jesus, who, by reason of the hypostatic union, was both human and divine.

Thanks to Jesus our *potentia obedientialis* is also actuated and we are "divinized" in the center of our being by the presence of God with whom we are united. And in the mystical life this is not mere theory but a tremendous reality to which one must constantly return through recollection and prayer. That is why the author of *The Cloud* can say: "Hold yourself at the sovereign point of the spirit . . ." And this teaching is profoundly biblical. For in the fourth gospel we hear Jesus speak constantly of the divine indwelling and of how he and the Father are present in the depth of our being. "If any man loves me, he will keep my word, and my Father will love him, and we will come to him and make our home with him." (John 14:23)

As for St. John of the Cross, he loves to speak of the center and his powerful little poem *The Living Flame of Love* opens with the mystical cry:

> O Living Flame of Love
> That tenderly wounds my soul
> In its deepest center[14]

In his commentary the Spanish mystic explains that the center of the soul is God and that the mystical life is a movement towards this deepest of centers. But the center of the soul is also human—it is the meeting place of the human and the divine.

Furthermore, St. John of the Cross comes close to Zuigan when he says that at the deepest center there is no deceit. He makes this point poetically by telling us that the bridal bed is "our flowery bed, encompassed with dens of lions . . ." Dens of lions, he explains, are very safe and protected against all other animals; and of this center he adds that "not only does the devil fail to find entry, but nothing in the world, high or low, is able to disquiet, molest, or even move the soul."[15]

Again, of this center St. John of the Cross, following the Christian tradition, says that it is "secret" or "hidden," that is to say, it is inaccessible to the senses and the intellect. One cannot be aware of it by reflection on one's activity in the manner I spoke of in my chapter self-realization. One can only be aware of it through mystical experience, which is a gift and a grace. And my reader will immediately observe how this parallels the Buddhist doctrine that everyone is enlightened but does not know it and that enlightenment is not the acquisition of some new knowledge but the realization of what has always been there.

Enough about the center. I will return to it again. Here it is sufficient to make the point that this center is not physically located in any determined part of the body nor is it in some realm of pure spirit. It pertains to the transformed body. Let me put it this way. One could say that when I enter deeply into the center of my being I reject the material and come to a realm of pure spirit where I meet God—this, however, is not the Christian approach. Or one could say that I enter into the depth of my being to the point where the human meets the divine and that, in doing so, matter is transformed—this is the Christian approach.

V

One last word about body language. I believe that the most powerful body language was spoken by Jesus when he was nailed to the cross.

And the same crucified body has spoken to millions of believers who, in time of anguish, could do nothing but gaze at the crucifix. For the body of Jesus says something that cannot be put into conceptual language. It says something about suffering and about love, something that cannot be said in any other way. And, after Jesus, thousands of Christian martyrs have spoken in the same way through their bodies. They have spoken without words; their blood has spoken.

And what of the risen body of Jesus? Has it spoken also? And what has it said?

The risen body of Jesus has reached the final stage of transformation. It is not confined to this place or to that. It was sown a physical body, it was raised a spiritual body. But, it speaks through millions of faithful human bodies and through the material universe when every tongue confesses "that Jesus Christ is Lord, to the glory of God the Father" (Phil. 2:11).

The Body of Christ

I

From what has been said it will already be clear that in the Christian mystical tradition the transformation of the human body has always been associated with the body of Christ. As Jesus died and rose, so we die and rise. As his body was transfigured, so ours will be transfigured. For Jesus, while being divine, is also one of us. He is, in Paul's words, "the first fruits of those who have fallen asleep" (1 Cor. 15:20).

As for the precise nature of the transfigured body, Paul, when asked about this, exclaims almost impatiently: "You foolish man! What you sow does not come to life unless it dies" (1 Cor. 15:36). And then he goes on to indicate that there are many kinds of matter and numerous modes of existence: "There is one kind for man, another for animals, another for birds, and another for fish. There are celestial bodies and there are terrestrial bodies. . . . There is one glory of the sun, and another glory of the moon, and another glory of the stars; for star differs from star in glory" (1 Cor. 15:39–41). It is as though Paul were saying: "There are limitless possibilities in the mind of God. And one more mode of existence is that of the risen body. But, you foolish man, you cannot understand it. So don't ask foolish questions!"

But some things are clear. And one is that our transformation through resurrection does not take place suddenly at the moment of death. It begins now. He who believes in Jesus has (not "will have") eternal life and Jesus will raise him up on the last day (John 6:54). It begins, moreover, with baptism, the great *metanoia* in which we die and rise to new life. For we are, in Paul's extraordinary words, baptized into Christ and baptized into his death.

But it is above all through the Eucharist that our flesh is transformed into his flesh and our body into his body. This was the doctrine of the primitive Christian community that took quite literally the words of Jesus in the fourth gospel: "He who eats my flesh and drinks my blood has eternal life and I will raise him up at the last day" (John 6:54). Flesh and blood here applies to the body of the Risen Jesus who will be with us all days to the end of the world. Into this Risen Jesus the believer is transformed through reception of the sacrament. One becomes Christ while remaining oneself; one is transformed into Christ while retaining one's name. And all this is a pledge, a foretaste, a preparation for the great event that is his second coming: "I will raise him up at the last day" (John 6:54). At that time the transformation not only of the human body but of the whole universe will be complete. Because there will be a new heaven and a new earth (Rev. 21:1). Obviously we are here in the realm of mysticism where words become inadequate.

And it is interesting to listen to the church fathers talk about the transformation of the human person into Christ. They are careful to make one point: That whereas when we eat ordinary bread we transform it into ourselves, when we eat the bread of life that is Jesus we are transformed into him. That is why St. Leo can write in the fifth century: "Participation in the Body and Blood of Christ produces in us none other effect than to make us pass into that which we take."[16] Even more remarkable is Augustine, who makes Jesus say: "I am the food of the strong; have faith and eat me. But thou wilt not change me into thyself, it is Thou who will be transformed into me."[17] And in the Middle Ages, Thomas Aquinas (whose mysticism springs directly from the Eucharist) can state with scholastic clarity: "He who assimilates corporal food transforms it into himself; this change repairs the losses of the organism and gives it necessary increase. But the eucharistic food, instead of being transformed into the one who takes it, transforms him into itself. It follows that the proper effect of the Sacrament is to transform us so much into Christ, that we can truly say: 'I live, now not I; but Christ liveth in me'."[18]

But, needless to say, this is not an automatic process like the consumption of ordinary food. All is based on faith and love. "The efficacy of this Sacrament," writes Thomas, "is to work a certain transformation of ourselves into Christ by the process of charity . . . the property of charity is to transform the one who loves into the object of his love."

In view of all this one can understand how the medieval mystical movement was nourished by the Eucharist. And this holds true for the Rhineland mystics—Eckhart, Tauler, Suso. It holds true for the fourteenth century English mystics, including the author of *The Cloud*. It holds true for Thomas à Kempis, whose *Imitatio Christi* inspires in the reader a reverent longing to receive the body and blood of Christ. Johannes Tauler (1300–1361) speaks for the whole medieval tradition when he tells the faithful that all their practices and devotions are no more than preparations for the Eucharist: "Your meditations may be as profound, as exalted, as devout as you like, you may practice every pious exercise you can manage, but all this is as nothing in comparison with the Blessed Sacrament. What men do may be godly, but this Sacrament is God himself. It is in this Sacrament that man is transformed by grace into God."[19] Through Tauler, the great Dominican mystic and disciple of Eckhart, the medieval mystical tradition here raises its voice and speaks to the world.

II

What I have said until now concerns the Eucharist as the sacred banquet and the memorial of the Last Supper. From the twelfth century, however, a new step was taken in eucharistic devotion when the custom of preserving the sacred host in the tabernacle for the adoration of the faithful became widespread. This custom originated, it seems, because of certain controversies about the moment and nature of the real presence and because of a great desire among the people to see the sacred host. The bishop of Paris decreed that after the consecration in the mass the host be elevated for the adoration of the faithful. This custom spread rapidly to all parts of Europe and by 1300 it was the general practice of the Latin church. Subsequently there arose devotion to the body of Christ (*corpus Christi*), benediction, visits to the Blessed Sacrament and like devotions.

In the sixteenth century the reformers were acutely aware of abuses in these customs, and today some Catholic theologians are less than enthusiastic about a eucharistic adoration that frequently separates the body of Christ from its sacramental context in the eucharistic meal.

But granted that there have been abuses, it must quickly be added that such abuses need not be there, and that the reservation of the Eucharist in the tabernacle has fostered Catholic prayer and mysticism in an incalculable way. For the Eucharist is the symbol of the presence of Christ in our midst—a symbol that contains the reality of Christ who said: "I am with you always, to the close of the age" (Matt. 28:20). It continues the Old Testament notion of the presence of Yahweh with his people and the glory of God which filled the temple. Small wonder that millions of Christians have enjoyed profound religious experience in the eucharistic presence. The beauty of that presence is exquisitely described by the anonymous medieval poet who composed that little gem *Jesu dulcis*. The *memory* of Jesus, he writes, is sweet and gives joy to the heart, but far, far sweeter than honey is the *presence* of Jesus. And so we have the contrast between *Jesu dulcis memoria* and *eius dulcis praesentia*.

The sense of presence is, indeed, one of the chief characteristics of Christian mysticism. And how many Christians have relished that presence, sweeter than honey, while kneeling before the tabernacle in churches throughout the world! While *tasting* Jesus (again those interior senses), they have looked into the mirror of the Eucharist where they have seen their own beauty and his beauty too. And this vision has given them ineffable peace and joy.

III

Now all this may sound somewhat pious, but it was profoundly meaningful to no less a person than Teilhard de Chardin, whose cosmic vision was based on the Eucharist. Recall that time when in prayer before the monstrance he saw the sacred host get bigger and bigger until it enveloped the whole earth. Teilhard then understood that through the body of Christ not only the human race but the whole earth is "Christified" and sanctified. Then there is Teilhard's mass of the universe wherein he felt deeply the cosmic dimension of the body of Christ. And all this was linked for him with the spiritual power of matter and the power of the Eucharist to divinize the earth.

For as Jesus is divine so the human race is divinized by his body. This is an idea that is deeply rooted in the teachings of the church fathers. Irenaeus, Clement, Athanasius and Gregory of Nyssa all speak about the "divinization" or "deification" of man. Augustine does not hesitate to use the Latin *deificari;* Origen uses the Greek Θεοποιεῖσθαι; and until after Augustine we find constant appeal to the saying "God became man in order that man might become God." It is true, of course, that the fathers, aware of the dangers inherent in such language, condemn the idea that man is part of God or that he is "consubstantial with God." But there can be no doubt about the Christian tradition that as Jesus is son by nature we are sons and daughters by grace. Through him we are adopted children; we are sharers in the divine nature. "Through the mystery of this water and wine may we come to share in his divinity who humbled himself to share in our humanity."[20] I recall how a Buddhist who attended a Christian Eucharist asked me afterwards if we really grasped the full implications of these words.

IV

I have spoken about the divinization of the human race and about the remarkable mysticism that lies at the heart of Christianity. I believe that it is all true. I believe that God became man in order that man might become God. However, we must never be so mesmerized by this glorious teaching as to forget the other side of the picture. We must never forget that we who are divinized are also weak, weak human beings. We must never forget Unmon's shit-stick, for that is what we are. And if we overlook this obvious truth we may have a rude awakening when we fall flat on our faces in the mud. Something like this may have happened to St. Paul. To keep him from being too elated by the abundance of revelations, a thorn was given him in the flesh, a messenger of Satan, to harass him. And Paul realized that the good he wanted to do he did not do, but the evil he wished to avoid was what he did. We all have the same experience, particularly when our *hubris* grows so great that we forget our weakness.

V

But let me end with an important corollary.

What I have said about the Eucharist and the divinization of the human race is taken largely from the Catholic tradition, and I ask myself if it will appeal to my Protestant brothers and sisters. For it is undeniable that since the Reformation and the religious upheaval of the sixteenth century, Catholic and Protestant prayer and devotion have developed along different lines. While Protestant devotion has been profoundly biblical, the Catholic Church has tried to maintain its eucharistic mysticism and, in general, has succeeded in so doing, particularly in its monasteries and religious congregations.

But we are now entering a new religious era, an era in which the most important event will be the meeting between Christianity and the great religions of the East. In this era, it is imperative that the Catholic and Protestant devotional traditions should dialogue and share their treasures. Together we must create a truly biblical mysticism that will speak with confidence to the mystical traditions of Hinduism and Buddhism.

NOTES

1. Tomio Hirai, M.D., *Zen and the Mind* (Tokyo: Japan Publications, 1978), p. 51 ff. Dr. Hirai writes: "Prolonging exhalation is one way to reduce the number of breaths. One should exhale very slowly and so gently that the flow of air would not disturb a feather attached to the tip of the nose. At the end of the exhalation, air will be inhaled quickly into the lungs."
2. Dr. Hirai says that the measured chanting of the Buddhist sutras makes the breath rhythmical. The same, I believe, can be said of Gregorian chant in traditional Christian monasticism. Dr. Hirai suggests that a phrase from a piece of poetry or a song repeated in a fixed pattern makes the breath rhythmical.

3. Anthony de Mello, *Sadhana: A Way to God* (St. Louis: Institute of Jesuit Sources, 1978), p. 24.
4. Katsuki Sekida, trans., *Two Zen Classics: Mumonkan and Hekigan-roku* (Tokyo: Weatherhill, 1977), p. 29.
5. Shunryu Suzuki, *Zen Mind, Beginners Mind* (Tokyo: Weatherhill, 1970), p. 25.
6. Mircea Eliade, *Yoga: Immortality and Freedom* (Princeton, NJ: Princeton University Press, 1969), p. 56.
7. Ibid.
8. See Diana Mary Law, "The Breath of Contemplative Prayer in East and West" (M.A. thesis, Sophia University, 1979).
9. John K. Ryan, trans., *The Confessions of St. Augustine* (New York: Doubleday, 1960), Bk. 10, c. 6.
10. *The Living Flame of Love*, st. 4.
11. Ibid., commentary on st. 4.
12. *Mumonkan*, Case 12.
13. Bede Griffiths, *Return to the Center* (Springfield, IL: Templegate, London: Collins, 1976).
14. *The Living Flame of Love*, st. 1.
15. Ibid., Commentary on st. 1.
16. *Sermo 63 de Passione*, 12, c. 7.
17. *Confessions*, L. vii, c. 4.
18. *In IV Sentent.*, Dist. 12 q.2, a.1.
19. John Tauler, O.P., *Spiritual Conferences* (St. Louis: Herder, 1961), p. 269.
20. Prayer from the mass.

4

Words and Silence

W ISE OLD QOHELETH reminds us that there is "a time to keep silence and a time to speak" (Eccles. 3:7). And his good advice holds true not only for human relationships but also for our relationship with God. There are times when we pour forth words from the depth of our being; and there are those other times when we remain silent.

Some people who are willing to use words and phrases in prayer are less convinced of the value of silence. Let them listen to another wise old sage, Lao-tsu, who declares that "silence is the great revelation." It is as though he were saying that not only through words but also through silence do we come to understand the great mystery that surrounds our life. Anyone who has meditated simply by preserving deep silence of mind and heart knows that this is true, for in attentive silence one becomes aware of one's body, of ones thoughts, of one's feelings, of one's deepest self—and when the silence really deepens, one becomes aware of an obscure sense of presence that lies at the heart of the universe and at the center of one's being. Truly, silence is the great revelation; and let no one deny that it is so.

But let me begin by discussing the role of words in the great journey to enlightenment. And after that I will speak about the tension between words and silence in the same great journey.

The Way of Words

I

In some of the great religions one can pray simply by repeating the name of God. This practice is beautifully conspicuous in Hinduism, where the thousand names of God are often memorized and recited by the devout believer. Each name emphasizes one special attribute of the divinity. Anthony de Mello has adapted this practice to Christian prayer, and he suggests that one invent a thousand names for Jesus and repeat them lovingly in prayer. "I propose that you now invent a thousand names for Jesus. Imitate the psalmist who is not satisfied with the usual names of God like Lord, Savior, King, but with the creativity that comes from a heart full of love invents names for God. *You are my rock*, he will say, *my shield, my fortress, my delight, my song* . . ."[1] This is an excellent use of words in prayer.

Again, in Hinduism and Buddhism we have the *mantra*, which is primarily a sound and is defined as follows in a standard Buddhist dictionary:

> Originally in Brahmanism and Hinduism, a syllable, word or verse which was revealed to a seer in meditation. An embodiment in sound of a power which can effect spiritual and sometimes temporal results. Occasionally it is regarded as an embodiment in sound of a deity.[2]

Here it is worth noting that the *mantra* is "revealed to a seer in meditation." It is not discovered in a dictionary but wells up from the deep unconscious layers of the psyche during meditation. For this reason it is holy and sacred—it is an embodiment of power and sometimes an embodiment of a deity.

In this context, however, we must carefully distinguish between a word that is truly religious and one that is magical. In authentic religion the power of the word resides not in the sound itself but in the faith of the speaker. In magic, on the other hand, the power resides in the word itself—hence what counts is the correct formula, correctly pronounced, and this formula must be kept a dark secret, since anyone who knows it automatically possesses the power. It is this magical use of words (as well as the mechanical recitation of sounds) that Jesus castigates when he says: "And in praying do not heap up empty phrases as the Gentiles do; for they think that they will be heard for their many words" (Matt. 6:7). And Jesus goes on to say that what matters is not the words but the faith: "For your Father knows what you need before you ask him" (Matt. 6:8). I emphasize this because magical formulas have been used in certain forms of oriental meditation that have been introduced to the West, and magic is to be avoided by one who would practice authentic religion.

Quite different from magic is the use of the name in the so-called Buddhism of faith. Here one recites the name of Amida lovingly and with great trust. The great Shinran (1173–1262) went so far as to say that if at the moment of death one is unable to recite the name, then faith in Amida will suffice to liberate him or her from bad *karma* and to ensure rebirth in the pure land. So important is faith—faith in Amida who has vowed (thereby uttering a word that resounds to the ends of the universe) that all who trust in him will be saved.

Very similar to calling on the name of the Buddha is the famous Jesus prayer, which has always held an honored place in orthodox spirituality and has recently spread rapidly to the whole Christian world. This prayer consists in repeating the name of Jesus with faith. Any name of Jesus will do (it need not necessarily be the word "Jesus") and one can either make one's own formula or use the standard formula of the orthodox church: "Lord Jesus, Son of God, have mercy on me a sinner." One comes to relish the name of Jesus and to love it. And, of course, the New Testament witnesses to the power of this name, as in that scene where Peter says to the lame man: "In the name of Jesus of Nazareth, walk" (Acts 3:6). And later Peter again affirms the power of this faith: "And his name, by faith in his name, has made this man strong whom you see and know." (Acts 3:16).[3]

Another Christian word of immense significance is *Abba*. This probably was the very word uttered by the lips of Jesus when he addressed his heavenly Father. He told us to use the same word when we betake ourselves to prayer. Already in this book I have spoken of how Paul feels that the Spirit unites himself to his spirit and cries out: "Abba, Father!" It is as though the word *Abba* were wrenched from the core of his being by the Holy Spirit who intercedes with sighs too deep for words (Rom. 8:26).

I have spoken of the words *Jesus* and of *Abba*, but it sometimes happens that one's personal word is revealed during quiet meditation or unexpectedly during the day. It simply rises up from the hidden depths, and one immediately knows that this is one's very own word. It may be a phrase from the scriptures like: "It is I; do not be afraid" (John 6:20), or it may be a single word. Such words are archetypal and express the cry of one's deepest self.

Again, one may use words in prayer by repeating and relishing the words of scripture, any words that appeal to one's soul. And these words may become so interiorized that they repeat themselves in the depths of one's being or rise up at unexpected times. It is as though they get into one's body and one's nervous system and one's very blood—and then one's whole being is talking and using words.

Another interesting use of words is found in the so-called *jubilatio* about which Augustine and Gregory the Great and other church fathers write. This is a form of speaking or singing or uttering sounds that contain no conceptual meaning but are extremely meaningful. This use of words is compared to the yodeling of the shepherds in the hills. The word *jubilatio* itself means "loud shouting" or "whooping" and it includes sighs and tears and gesticulations and other forms of body language. This way of praying, which almost disappeared in the Western church, has once more blossomed in our day among people who speak in tongues—in *glossolalia*. Properly understood it is a transcending of systematic reasoning and thinking and rationalizing to enter a deeper, more intuitive layer of the psyche.

II

In all these cases the word is extremely powerful. In the form of the prayer of petition, it can move mountains. In the form of the prayer of trust, it can fill us with gentle peace. In the form of a blessing, it can impart ineffable consolation to others. In the form of a curse, it can shrivel up strong men and valiant women, reducing them to the state of the withered fig tree. The word or mantra, repeated, repeated, repeated, until it is engraved on the tablets of the mind has incredible motive power; it can heal, it can transfigure, it can transform.

The Hebrews thought that the word had a substantial existence of its own; once uttered (like that great blessing of Isaac) it could never be recalled. And the oriental tradition in a somewhat similar vein speaks of *karma*, the word or thought that is like the pebble thrown into the pond, creating ripples and ripples and ripples throughout the universe.[4] Small wonder that Jesus warns us to be careful about our use of words: "Let what you say be simply 'Yes' or 'No'; anything more than this comes from evil" (Matt. 5:37).

But words operate at various levels of the psyche, and I would now like to discuss the interplay of words and silence in the mystical life.

The Way of Silence

I

The path of meditation, particularly of Christian meditation, ordinarily begins with words. These words may consist in the instruction we receive from a teacher or a book. Or in the meditation itself one may use words from the scriptures or one may use those words that arise spontaneously in the heart. One cries out to God in petition or thanksgiving or adoration. Or it may be that one uses the so-called discursive prayer of reasoning and thinking and conceptualization— one ponders on the truths of faith or the teaching of the Bible and then one cries out again to the Lord God of Heaven, asking for help or expressing one's gratitude.

But as prayer and meditation develop, the whole process usually begins to simplify. One may be content to repeat a single word like the word "Jesus." Or one may use a favorite ejaculation like "Come, Holy Spirit," repeated easily and quietly with the breathing or at one's own pace. And then the time may come when one prefers to use no words at all but simply *to be:* to be silent in the presence of the mystery. In such a state of prayer one may be unable to think because one is caught up in a peaceful wordlessness that is filled with love.

It is now that one enters the mystical silence, the *silentium mysticum* about which the Christian mystics love to talk. Now one enters the cloud of unknowing wherein one loves but does not discursively know; now one puts a cloud of forgetting between self and all the created things in the world; now one remains in the darkness, the emptiness, the quiet. Of course the imagination (St. Teresa calls it "the fool of the house") may romp wildly and uncontrollably, but one pays no attention to it, one lets it be—in order to remain at peace at the core of one's being.

In this silence the mystics speak of maintaining a certain *awareness*, that is to say, a certain attentiveness to the presence of God who is within or around. And for them this "obscure sense of presence" is a great grace. The old theologians spoke of it as a presence through love, in this way distinguishing it from physical presence or presence through knowledge. It is indeed *loving awareness*. [5]

One may retain this awareness constantly for a long time, indeed for many years. But if one preseveres it may happen that this loving awareness disappears and one is aware of nothing. One is left in nothingness. And this is the *nada* of the Spanish mystics. Nothing, nothing, nothing. The sense of presence has given way to a sense of absence.

And so, just as one must eventually abandon the breathing for breathing of another kind, so one must abandon the loving awareness for awareness of another kind. As there is breathing that is not breathing, so there is awareness that is not awareness, and there is a way that is no way. Concretely, one goes to prayer or meditation just to be there in pure or naked faith which is like night to the soul. Without words or ideas, without breathing, without even awareness I am *just sitting*. This can be a desert experience, an agonizing experience, an almost intolerable experience. For one feels quite helpless. This was the time when Teresa impatiently shook the hour glass (that medieval substitute for a clock), hoping that the sand would flow through quickly and bring her prayer to an end.

II

All this is silence, sometimes a bitter silence. But if one perseveres, it may happen that words or a word will rise up out of the silence; from the very depth of the unconscious there may arise a word to which, *pace* the exegetes, one can accommodate the text of Wisdom that says: "For while gentle silence enveloped all things, the night in its swift course was now half-gone, thy all-powerful word leaped from heaven . . ." (Wisd. 18:14,15).

This word that comes from inside is not necessarily an uttered word, though in some cases it is clearly spoken. Sometimes it is in the nature of a "stirring" (the term used by the anonymous author of *The Cloud*) or an inner movement, one pregnant with meaning. Sometimes it is just one word; at other times there is a succession of words.[6]

And so we find in meditation a cyclic process. One begins with words, which give way to silence; and the silence, in turn, gives birth to words; and the words to silence once more. I like to describe this in terms of *yin* and *yang*, those principles of Chinese philosophy to which I have already referred. Let me, then, say a word about *yin* and *yang*.

As is well known, the notions of *yin* and *yang* are the warp and woof of Chinese philosophy, so old that no one knows precisely where or when they originated. *Yin* stands for the feminine, intuitive mind, in our case, for the silence. *Yang*, on the other hand, is the rational, masculine intellect; it is the logos.

Yang, the masculine, is the sun and is represented by the character:

The same character stands for light and for heaven and for the head.

Yin, the feminine, is the moon and is represented by the character:

The same character stands for the shade and for the earth and for the belly.

The overall principle is that just as the sun when it reaches its zenith begins to decline, and just as the moon when it reaches its fullness begins to wane, so according to the principle of *enantio-dromia*, when the development of anything brings it to one extreme, a reversal to the other extreme takes place. This again is represented by the famous *T'ai-chi-T'u* or Diagram of the Supreme Ultimate:

As can be seen, the seed of light is in the darkness and the seed of darkness is in the light.

Applying all this to meditation we can understand how, when words become abundant and reach their fullness or saturation point, silence ensues. And out of the deep silence emerge words. It is a normal process, and the one who meditates should allow it to take place, never doing violence to self. One should never make efforts to abandon words and to enter the void. Neither should one disturb the void in order to form words. Do not awaken love before its time. Let the contemplative process unfold smoothly and quietly at its own pace and in its own time.

But now let me say something more about these words that arise out of the teeming womb of the void.

The Deeper Words

I

Let me preface my remarks with the reminder that St. John of the Cross is extremely wary and distrustful of all words. And his reasons are profoundly theological. He does not deny that words may proceed from the Holy Spirit and that they may be of great value; but he is deeply aware that God is the mystery of mysteries whose infinity no human word can understand or explain. He is aware that all human words, even those that are true, are imperfect and inadequate. Those who think that their human words contain the total reality of God are hopelessly deceived. For God can be known only by faith which is like night to the soul. With this in mind let me consider his approach to mystical words which he divides into three: *successive words*, *formal words* and *substantial words*.

Successive words may look like a return to the old discursive prayer, a return to the ordinary reasoning and thinking and consideration of the scriptures. For the person who has spent some time in the void, in the darkness, in the silent inability to think now finds that he or she can think and reason once again. But now he or she does so with a remarkable clarity because, in the terminology of St. John of the Cross, the spirit has been *illumined and purified*. The mind, which is ordinarily fettered and cramped by desire and fear, is now liberated. It may be capable not only of clear reasoning but also of clairvoyance, telepathy, the reading of hearts and other forms of extrasensory perception. This is altogether a normal development. But St. John of the Cross warns his readers that the dangers of deceit are very great in this area, and one must always have a healthy distrust of one's intuitions.

At this time, in deep recollection, there may also arise successive words that seem to proceed not from oneself but from some other person. Of these words St. John of the Cross writes: "A person will reason about his subject, proceeding thought by thought, forming precise words and judgments, deducing and discovering some unknown truth, with so much ease and clarity, that it will seem to him he is doing nothing and that another person is interiorly reasoning, answering, and teaching him."[7]

This is the time when some people engage in automatic writing, claiming that the Holy Spirit or some departed soul is guiding them and dictating what they should say. But St. John of the Cross (and here he represents the whole Christian mystical tradition) is adamantly opposed to such procedure. "I know someone who in his experience of these successive locutions formed, among some very true and solid ones about the Blessed Sacrament, others that were outright heresies."[8] And he continues with a warning that could be directed to many people in our day:

> And I greatly fear what is happening in these times of ours. If any soul whatever, after a bit of meditation, has in its recollection one of these locutions, it will immediately baptize all as coming from God and with such a supposition say, "God told me," "God answered me." Yet this is not so, but . . . these persons themselves are more often the origin of their locutions.[9]

Of course these persons are the origin of their locutions. For these words are coming not indeed from the ego but from the self, that vast, undiscovered, uncharted world that is our total being and is unknown to our own ego.[10]

But the Spanish saint goes further and speaks of the possibility of demonic interference. Anyone with a little experience in these matters knows that this is very real—that one may meet the devil in the deeper layers of the psyche. And frequently it is very, very difficult to detect the demonic presence because the evil one transforms himself into an angel of light. Be that as it may, St. John of the Cross concludes that "we should pay no attention to them (i.e., successive words) but be only interested in firmly directing the will through them to God."[11]

Next come *formal words*. These differ from successive words in that they may arise suddenly in the mind at any time of the day or night—not necessarily in the time of deep recollection:

> Sometimes these words are very explicit and at other times not. They are like ideas spoken to the spirit, either as a reply to something or in another manner. At times only one word is spoken, and then again more than one; sometimes the locutions are successive, like the others, for they may endure while the soul is being taught, or while something is being discussed. All these words come without any intervention of the spirit, because they are received as though one person were speaking to another.[12]

Once again, while the Spanish mystic concedes that the origin of these words may well be the Holy Spirit (they may pertain to the gift of prophecy) he is, nevertheless, wary about accepting them as valid. They should be manifested to a discreet person, and if such a person cannot be found it is better not to speak about these words at all and not to pay attention to them. Elsewhere, while speaking of prophecy, St. John of the Cross distinguishes between the divine communication which is true and the human interpretation which may be false. He speaks relentlessly of the many good people in both the old and the new dispensation who have been deceived by prophecy. And so he concludes that "in this matter of locutions strange and subtle deceits will occur—so much so that I believe a person who is unopposed to them cannot but be deceived. . ."[13]

The only interior word to which St. John of the Cross gives unqualified approval is the *substantial word*. To understand this one must recall that by substance he here means the center of the soul about which I have spoken at length. The substantial word is the word that issues from this deep center where the human touches and mingles with the divine and where no deceit can occur. This is the area to which no demonic force can penetrate; it is the area that is ordinarily hidden even from ourselves.[14] And the saint makes the extraordinary statement that the word rising from these hidden depths "does more good for a person than a whole lifetime of deeds."[15]

And the chief characteristic of the word is that, "vital and substantial," it accomplishes what it intends. "For example, if Our Lord should say formally to the soul, 'Be good,' it would immediately be substantially good; or if He should say, 'Love me,' it would immediately have and experience within itself the substance of the love of God; or if He should say to a soul in great fear, 'Do not fear,' it would without delay feel ample fortitude and tranquillity."[16]

Here there can be no deceit. Yet I must recount one disturbing reservation that the saint makes. He jolts the reader when he states that the devil is incapable of producing these locutions in the soul "unless, as it may happen, the soul has surrendered itself to him by a voluntary pact."[17] Here we are up against evil in a big way.

Aside from this, however, there can be no deception. Moreover, there are degrees of interiority and substantiality. One can go on and on and on into the substance of the soul where man meets God.

II

As can readily be seen, St. John of the Cross is a first-class radical. He is satisfied only with the deepest experience which issues from the core of one's being, and he tends to brush aside the more superficial movements of the psyche. And this he can do because he is a contemplative writing for contemplatives. St. Ignatius, on the other hand, is an active person directing active persons, and he is anxious to discern the more superficial movements of the psyche. His *Rules for the Discernment of Spirits*, though they do not explicitly mention words, help us to discern the validity of successive and formal words —help us to discern whether or not we should base our actions on these inner words. For Ignatius analyzes in great detail the inner movements, pointing out which are neurotic (if I may put it in modern terminology) and which are healthy, which lead to good and which lead to evil, which lead to life and which lead to death, which are from God and which are from the evil one.

Yet Ignatius is at one with St. John of the Cross in affirming that there is a center at which no deceit is possible, a center of radical immediacy to God; this is the center wherein one experiences "consolation without previous cause." He writes:

> It belongs to God alone to give consolation without previous cause, for it belongs to the Creator to enter into the soul, to leave it, and to act upon it, drawing it wholly to the love of His Divine Majesty. I say without previous cause, that is, without any previous perception or knowledge of any object from which such consolation might come to the soul through its own acts of intellect and will.[18]

Here is the Ignatian way of judging whether or not a word issues from the substance or center of the soul. Consolation without previous cause is a sign of the direct action of God. His *Spiritual Exercises* lead the exercitant to experience such consolation and in this way to come to a decision in which there can be no deceit.

In his *Spiritual Journey*, moreover, Ignatius distinguishes between interior words (*loqüela interna*) which arise from the center, the substantial area about which we have been speaking, and exterior words (*loqüela externa*) which arise from a more superficial layer of the psyche. The *loqüela interna* come "more slowly, more interiorly, gently without noise or notable movements, coming apparently from within, without knowing how to explain them."[19] This beautiful description helps us to discern the substantial word that comes to us gently and delicately like a drop of water entering a sponge.

III

But does the cyclic process of words-silence-words-silence-words-silence go on forever? Just as the *yin* and the *yang* proceed from the Tao, is there a final reality from which all words and silence flow?

I believe that there is a final word, and this is the WORD INCARNATE who dwells in the depth of our being through baptism and the Eucharist. St. John of the Cross describes how, at the peak point of the mystical life, the WORD awakens:

> How gently and lovingly
> You wake in my heart
> Where in secret you dwell alone.[20]

Here we have the final word arising in the center and substance of the soul. It is the personalized WORD; it is Jesus himself, to whom St. John of the Cross can cry: "How gentle and loving is Your awakening, O Word, Spouse, in the center and depth of my soul, which is its pure and intimate substance, in which secretly and silently, as its only Lord, You dwell alone . . . ."[21] And he goes on to speak of this awakening of the WORD in astonishing terms: "For this awakening is a movement of the Word in the substance of the soul, containing such grandeur, dominion and glory, and intimate sweetness that it seems to the soul that all the balsams and fragrant spices and flowers of the world are commingled, stirred and shaken so as to yield their sweet odor, and that all the kingdoms and dominions of the world and all the powers and virtues of heaven are moved . . . ."[22]

IV

And so, in the cyclic movement of words and silence, the final reality is the WORD. The Word made flesh awakens in the substance of the soul and cries out: "Abba, Father!" And in this way is effected the divinization of the human person through the grace of Jesus Christ.

In this way are fulfilled those words of the gospel: "But to all who received him, who believed in his name, he gave power to become children of God" (John 1:12). Through baptism and the Eucharist one becomes a child of God; through mystical experience one comes to realize existentially that this is so. Mystical experience is a profound realization of what we are and of the grace we already possess.

It is all very true and very beautiful. But even as we speak of these great realities we must never forget our own weakness. We must never forget Unmon's dried shit-stick. With Paul we can only glory in our weakness and realize that we are nothing.

Body Language

Earlier in this book I spoke about zen Buddhism's distrust of words and letters; I said that zen rejects theory and conceptualization in a very radical way. But this does not mean that zen rejects words of every kind. Zen, far from rejecting language, has developed an extremely powerful body language through which there is a direct communication from mind to mind. This communication one might call "intersubjective." And without it zen would rightly be called quietistic, negative and passive. Since I have already spoken about this intersubjective language I will not treat of it in detail here. Only let me quote one zen koan that illustrates the power of the body in the relationship between master and disciple.

Zen Master Gutei, after his great enlightenment, never spoke again. He did, however, direct disciples; and he did so by simply raising his finger. Hence his way was called "one-finger zen." Now there was a servant boy in the temple, and a visitor asked him: "How does your master teach zen?" And the boy, mimicking his master, raised his finger. At this moment Master Gutei appeared at the door and, seeing the boy, he ran forward and cut off his finger with a knife. Screaming with pain the boy ran away. Whereupon Gutei called out to him: "Hey!" As the boy turned around, Gutei raised his finger. And the boy was enlightened.

What powerful body language we find here! First of all, there is the finger of Gutei. So deeply enlightened is the master that conceptual words will not express what is in his mind. And so he has resort to another kind of word: he throws his whole body, his whole self, into the uplifted finger. And in this action there is a direct communication between his self and the self of the disciple—a direct communication that triggers off enlightenment.

As for his seemingly cruel action in cutting off the boy's finger, a colleague of mine who passed this koan with a master told me that in identifying with Gutei he understood as if for the first time the words of Jesus: "And if your right hand causes you to sin, cut it off and throw it away . . ." (Matt. 5:30). For just as we ask, "How could a compassionate zen master perform such a cruel act?" so we might say, "How could the compassionate Jesus say such a bloodthirsty thing?"

And one can understand the words of Jesus only when one identifies with the Jesus who embraced the cross and, in this sense, cut off his own right hand. In this bloody way he showed his compassion towards the whole human family and pointed the way towards that great enlightenment which is resurrection.

NOTES

1. Anthony de Mello, *Sadhana: A Way to God* (St. Louis: Institute of Jesuit Sources, 1978), p. 112.
2. *Japanese-English Buddhist Dictionary* (Tokyo: Daito Shuppansha, 1965).
3. One can distinguish between the *name* of Jesus, of which there is only one, and the *titles*, of which there are many. Each of the titles is an access to some aspect of the mystery of the name.
4. *Karman* is defined as "a deed which is produced by the action of the mind. *Karman*, when manifested, is produced either verbally or physically . . . that which is produced by the mind, body or mouth (i.e., words), and which will produce an effect in the future" (*Japanese-English Buddhist Dictionary*). In Buddhism, Judaism and Christianity the classic example of a word that cannot be recalled is the vow. Remember the sad story of Jepthah: "Alas, my daughter! You have brought me very low, and you have become the cause of great trouble to me; for I have opened my mouth to the Lord, and I cannot take back my vow" (Judg. 11:35). A similar way of thinking may have been in the mind of Herod when he kept his terrible promise to Salome and beheaded John the Baptist.
5. Though zen speaks much of awareness I have not found any reference in zen to the "obscure sense of presence." I have sometimes asked zen masters about the sense of presence but I have not yet found any who recognize it or consider it of any value.
6. "By the word is meant any expression of religious meaning or of religious value. Its carrier may be intersubjectivity, or art, or symbol, or language, or the remem-

bered and portrayed lives or deeds or achievements of individuals or classes or groups." Bernard Lonergan, *Method in Theology* (New York: Seabury; London: Darton, Longman and Todd, 1972, p. 112.)

7. *Ascent*, Bk. 2, c. 29.
8. Ibid., p. 207.
9. Ibid.
10. St. John of the Cross maintains that interior words and inspirations may come from one of three sources: the Holy Spirit, the evil spirit, or one's self. He was, however, educated in a theology that clearly separated the natural and the supernatural and said (or, at least, indicated strongly) that what comes from one's self does not come from God. In the light of modern psychology and theology I would prefer to say that all these words and movements come from the self—as influenced either by God or by the spirit of evil.
11. *Ascent*, Bk. 2, c. 29.
12. Ibid., c. 30.
13. Ibid.
14. "Indeed, not only does the soul fail to understand, but no one understands, not even the devil, since the Master who teaches the soul *dwells within it substantially where neither the devil, the natural senses, nor the intellect can reach*" (*The Dark Night*, Bk. 11, c. 17).
15. *Ascent*, Bk. 2, c. 31.
16. Ibid.
17. Ibid.
18. *Spiritual Exercises of St. Ignatius*, Rules for Discernment of Spirits, Second Week, Rule 2.
19. See Harvey Egan, S.J., *The Spiritual Exercises and the Ignatian Mystical Horizon* (St. Louis: Institute of Jesuit Sources, 1976), p. 52.
20. *The Living Flame of Love* st. 4.
21. Ibid., commentary on st. 4.
22. Ibid.

5

The Holy Books

A LL THE GREAT religions have their holy books which believers love and cherish and in which they find inspiration, guidance and light. One has only to think of the Koran in Islam, of the Upanishads in Hinduism, of the sutras in Buddhism, of the Bible in Judaism and Christianity. Reading or listening to these books has been for millions of believers a powerful religious experience, a path to enlightenment, a way of salvation. Small wonder, then, that the holy books have always been treated with reverential love and have been accorded a place of honor in temple, in synagogue and in church. They have given inspiration not only to the splendid liturgies of all religions but also to great music like that of Handel, to great poetry like that of St. John of the Cross, to great painting and sculpture like that of Michelangelo, to great social movements like that of Mahatma Gandhi.[1]

Buddhism has an enormous number of scriptures, composed in many languages—in Pali, in Sanskrit, in Chinese, in Tibetan. The most complete corpus, edited in Japan in 1934, is in Chinese and consists of more than three thousand scriptures in one hundred volumes. Since it includes texts composed by Chinese and Japanese saints and scholars, one might compare it not to the Bible but to the

Bible together with the works of the church fathers and the early
Christian writers. Obviously, no one person can master all these
texts. Each Buddhist sect has its own special sutras within the total
corpus, and these it venerates and uses in liturgy and in worship.[2]

But if all believers reverence their scriptures, Jews and Christians
have special reason for so doing, in view of their belief that their holy
books were inspired by God himself. This doctrine of divine inspiration, though not taught explicitly in the Old Testament, was gradually elaborated within Judaism through the ages; it was said that the
Torah existed with God before the creation of the world and was
subsequently revealed to Moses. As for Christianity, the doctrine of
inspiration that appears in the New Testament was elaborated to the
point where the Christian community claimed (as it still claims) that
God himself is the author of its scriptures. Christians, furthermore,
believe that there is a certain presence of Christ in the words of
scripture, that one can meet Jesus in the perusal of the sacred text.
Indeed, Christian tradition speaks of a quasi-incarnation of the Word
in the sacred writings. Just as there is a union of the human and the
divine in Jesus, so there is a union of the human and the divine in
the Bible. But just as the union of the human and the divine in Jesus
is a mystery we will never understand, so also the union of the human
and the divine in the Bible will always baffle the human mind.

In all this, however, the point I wish to make is that the holy books
of the great religions were not written primarily to give information
but to bring the reader to conversion and salvation. The fourth gospel
makes this point well when the author declares that he could have
related all kinds of things about Jesus "but these are written that you
may believe that Jesus is the Christ, the Son of God, and that
believing you may have life in his name" (John 20:31). It is as though
he were to say: "I am writing this book to lead you to *metanoia* and
to salvation. If you read my book you may not only learn something,
you may find yourself profoundly changed."

Beautiful and inspiring as the holy books are, they became a source
of acute embarrassment to many Western men and women during the
first part of this century. Surely, it was thought, these books are filled
with myths and stories that are totally unacceptable to the scientific
mind. How is one to read them? What is one to make of them? And
the problem became all the more acute when the books themselves

were subjected to the rigors of a scientific research that pointed to their mythical dimension, leaving many believers shocked and perplexed.

And then Jung raised his prophetic voice in the wilderness with the cry that myth, far from being childish nonsense, is an essential ingredient in human psychological life. Human beings need myth and story no less than they need bread and rice. Without the great symbols provided by the holy books, men and women are like lost children; they are left without meaning, they are wandering in the dark. Jung went even further and declared that Western man was sick, desperately sick, because he had lost his myth. He begged Westerners to find their myth not by running to the East as "pitiable imitators" but by refinding the treasures that exist in their own tradition. He was criticized and even ridiculed by his contemporaries, but it seems now he has won the day.

For most thinking people now recognize the importance of myth and symbol in human life. If science is the *yang*, then myth is the *yin*. It is the belly. And it answers the deeper and darker questions about meaning, about suffering, about life after death, about good and evil, about God. Jung was far from denying the value of science. He knew well enough that we cannot be all belly and that we need a head. But he saw that the person who has no story to fall back on is desperately frustrated in time of suffering, whereas the person in whose psyche the story of the crucified God is vibrantly alive finds meaning in the cross. Like Paul he may even glory in the cross of Our Lord Jesus Christ.

And so, if we are searching for something that is common to the great religions, we find it in myth. The religions are telling us a story or stories that will nourish our unconscious, live in our archetypes, answer our deeper questions, give meaning to the riddle of life.

And yet, when we speak of Judaism and Christianity as myth we must pause for a moment, for these great religions claim that their holy books are not only myth but also history. Jews and Christians believe that God really chose a people and that he spoke through Abraham and Isaac and Jacob and the prophets. Obviously this does not mean that the Bible can be called critical history in our modern sense of this term. We know that it contains legend and poetry and fiction. But it does mean that the Bible recounts *saving events* and that the words describe and explain these events. And this is particularly important when we think of the life and death and resurrection of Jesus, which can be called *the Christ event*. Any historian of religions knows that death-and-resurrection is a basic myth, found all over the world, but Christians believe that in Jesus myth and history meet. Jesus is the great Christian symbol, but he is not only a symbol—he is a living reality. And Christians believe that when they look into the depth of their being they find not just the symbol of Jesus but the Risen Jesus himself. They believe that when Paul said, "It is no longer I who live but Christ who lives in me." (Gal. 2:20), he meant precisely what he said.

For this reason when we read the Judaeo-Christian scriptures we must pay attention not only to the symbolical, but also to the historical, dimension. This is a tremendous challenge. Put concretely, we must love and live the Christian myth while at the same time welcoming the scientific discoveries of historians and archaeologists and all those who speak about the events that took place in Palestine two thousand years ago. Just as we accept the humanity and the divinity of Jesus, so we accept the human and the divine authorship of the Bible. But in doing this (let us admit it frankly) we are sometimes led into a cloud of unknowing.

In this chapter, however, I have set myself a clear objective. I want to explore how we, Christian men and women of the twentieth century, should approach our holy books and read them so that they will perform their task of leading us to enlightenment and even to the peak point of the mystical life. To do this I will first look to the past, asking how Buddhists and Christians have read their scriptures, and then I will ask how we today can read them, benefiting from the experience of the past and from the wealth of scholarly research that has enriched us during recent decades.

The Way of Reading

I

The great religions have seen that if myth and symbol are to have motivating power they must come to life not just in the rational consciousness but in the deeper layers of the psyche. And so, teachers and believers have found ways of driving the sacred words into those dark depths and into the body itself. Let me first say a word about how the Buddhist tradition has done just this.

One of the most widely loved scriptures in East Asia is the Lotus Sutra.[3] This sutra, which speaks of the perfect enlightenment of the Buddha and of the possibility of enlightenment for everyone, is virtually worshipped in the Tendai and Nichiren sects of Buddhism. Followers of the Nichiren sect recite the words: *Namu-myōhō-renge-kyō* (Honor to the Lotus Sutra) again and again and again, until the formula burns into their deepest psyche and even into their body. This formula, moreover, they chant night and morning before a sacred scroll that hangs in the home. Believers transcribe it on a headband or on a sash that they wear across their bodies. And they believe that the constant recitation of these words has intercessory power to change the world.

Nichiren himself (1222–1282) had the most profound devotion to the Lotus Sutra about which he constantly spoke and preached. In a powerful little letter that he wrote just before going into exile in the island of Sado, he speaks about reading the Lotus Sutra with one's whole body. The letter, known as the "Dungeon Letter" is addressed to his favorite disciple Nichiro who was in prison for his faith. It runs as follows:

> Tomorrow I leave for Sado. With compassion I think of you in the dungeon on this cold night. Honorable Nichiro, if you are a man who realizes even part of the Lotus Sutra with both body and mind, you will bring salvation to your family, relatives, and all sentient beings. When some people read the Lotus Sutra, they mouth the words but don't read with the mind. And if they read with the mind, they don't read with the body. To read with both body and mind is the most exalted. It is written, "Angels will come and serve those who believe in the Lotus Sutra, and though dharma enemies may try to hurt them with knives or sticks or poison, they will never be able to do so," and so nothing terrible will happen to us. When you get out of prison please come to me at once. I want to see you, just as you want to see me.
>
> Humbly Yours,
> Nichiren

Eighth Year of Bun'ei (1271)
October 9th

As one can immediately see, this letter overflows with love for, and faith in, the Lotus Sutra. And note how Nichiren claims that proper recitation of this sutra is a way of salvation not only for Nichiro himself but also for his relatives and friends. And note again how, in a remark that reminds one of the psalmist, he declares that the person who recites the Lotus Sutra with faith will be marvelously protected from his enemies. But most interesting of all is his counsel to read the scripture with one's body. It is not sufficient to mouth the words nor even to understand them intellectually. One must read them with one's body. What does this mean?

It is clear that Nichiren opposes any mechanical gabbling of words, words, words. What he wants is a total commitment to the sutra, a commitment that embraces mouth and mind, bone and blood, breathing and body. Hence he uses the Japanese word *shindoku* meaning "body-reading." If one recites "Honor to the Lotus Sutra," one must do so with one's whole self and never with the lips alone.

And there is another way of body-reading the scriptures. One can sit splendidly in the lotus, regulate one's breathing, still one's mind and take the sacred words into one's deepest self, into one's belly. Then one simply sits with the text. There is no reasoning and thinking. One is simply present to the words, digesting the words, living the words. In this way one comes to *realize* the scriptures, not through rationalization, but through life.[4]

Or, again, one can dance the scriptures. Or one can copy them like the great Chinese and Japanese calligraphists or like the Celtic monks who wrote the *Book of Kells*. And this copying is no mere mechanical exercise; it is a bodily religious experience that leads to enlightenment.

Though the cultural background is vastly different, one finds a certain body-reading taught in the book of Deuteronomy where the Hebrews are told to repeat the words of Yahweh again and again and again, until these words enter the deep caverns of the unconscious. Here is the text:

> And these words which I command you this day shall be upon your heart; and you shall teach them diligently to your children, and shall talk of them when you sit in your house, and when you walk by the way, and when you lie down, and when you rise. And you shall bind them as a sign upon your hand, and they shall be as frontlets between your eyes.

And you shall write them on the doorposts of your house and on your gates. [Deut. 6:6–9]

Here is a command to take the words of Yahweh not only into the mind but into the body, into the belly, into the deep layers of the psyche. The sacred text must come alive within the Jewish people. The words of Yahweh must penetrate them through and through as they sit and as they walk and as they lie down. The words of Yahweh must penetrate their hands, their eyes, their doorposts, their gates. In short, the Jews must be saturated with the sacred words.

II

And in the Christian medieval tradition the same kind of approach is much in evidence. In the monasteries the monks chanted the psalms and the scriptures. Outside the monasteries, the faithful recited the rosary, thus praying not only with their minds, which contemplated the great biblical mysteries, but also with their lips and with their fingers.

And then there is the so-called *lectio divina* which was central to monastic piety. Here one takes a text of scripture and tastes and relishes it with those marvelous and delicate interior senses. One does not think or reason about the text, one does not reflect at all—one simply tastes and savors and allows the text to sink into one's being, to become part of oneself, to nourish one's inner life.

This approach to scripture was developed by St. Ignatius who taught a kind of meditation that he called "the application of the senses." He invites us to enter into the mysteries of Jesus and Mary— to see the scene, to listen to the persons, to smell the fragrance, to taste the sweetness, to touch and embrace and kiss the place where the persons stand or are seated. Here there is no hard-hearted rationalism; one is approaching the sacred books with one's heart and with one's senses.

Yet another way in which the Christian scriptures have been read is through dialogue with the sacred text. Jung, it is interesting to recall, did something like this with the *I Ching*. He personified the book, flipped the coins, and asked his question. His experiment was not, in my opinion, eminently successful, but it is significant that

such a great scholar should dialogue with a holy book in this way.
And a different kind of dialogue has been carried on by Christians
who, in time of stress, have asked the Bible for help. They have
glanced through the pages in search of an answer. And frequently
they have claimed that the Holy Spirit has made known to them what
they should do. In this way they have treated the Bible as a living
book.

III

And how the Judaeo-Christian tradition loves the notion of tasting
and eating the holy books! Perhaps this is because the sacred banquet
plays such a central role in biblical thought. The theme of *eating* the
scroll is found in Ezekiel and is replayed in the Apocalypse:

> And I took the little scroll from the hand of the angel and ate it; it was
> sweet as honey in my mouth, but when I had eaten it my stomach was
> made bitter. [Rev. 10:10]

I believe that these words describe a very real religious experience.
We can taste and relish the beautiful literature of the scriptures, and
we may find the words sweet as honey in our mouths, but when we
come to digest them, to live them, to prophesy and to do what they
tell us—then, indeed, our stomachs may become exceedingly bitter.
Then we may feel something like the birth pangs of a woman in
travail.

And the notion of eating the scroll (just as one eats the bread of
the Eucharist) found its way into the Christian liturgy and into the
mysticism of the Middle Ages, where we hear of the two tables: the
table of the Eucharist and the table of Holy Scripture. Thomas à
Kempis prays beautifully:

> You have given your holy body to strengthen my weak mind and body,
> and you have given your word for a lamp to guide my feet. Without these
> two things I cannot live as I ought; for the word of God is the light of
> my soul, and your Sacrament the bread that gives me life. They are like
> two tables, one on this side and one on that in the treasurehouse of holy
> Church. One table is the sacred altar with the holy bread, the precious
> body of Christ. The other is the Law of God containing the holy doc-
> trine. . . .[5]

The Second Vatican Council took up this theme and declared: "The Church has always venerated the divine Scriptures just as she venerates the Body of the Lord, since from the table of both the word of God and of the Body of Christ she unceasingly receives and offers to the faithful the bread of life. . . ."[6] And indeed in many Christian churches to this day one finds the two tables of which à Kempis speaks, the table of the Eucharist and the table of the Word. For these are the two sources of Christian spiritual life.

And so we are drawn to the conclusion that just as by the Eucharist the human person is divinized and becomes a child of God, so through the reading of sacred scripture the same process of divinization is effected. And this is the primary meaning of sacred scripture in the Christian life.

IV

From what I have said it will be clear that in Buddhism, Judaism and Christianity the person who would understand the holy books must be committed to them. And this brings us back once more to the doctrine of Augustine and Anselm: *Crede ut intelligas: Believe that you may understand.* You do not believe after you have understood, but through belief you get light and insight and understanding.

This point is particularly stressed in the Christian tradition which has always held that one cannot understand the sacred scriptures without the inner light of the Holy Spirit. When we believe and when we love, the Holy Spirit is given to us in accordance with those words of Jesus: "If you love me . . . I will pray the Father, and he will give you another Counselor, to be with you for ever, even the Spirit of truth . . ." (John 14:15–17). Yes, it is the Spirit who enlightens and gives understanding; without the Spirit we have no insight whatever. And this again is beautifully expressed by à Kempis.

> Prophets may employ words, but they do not give the spirit. They may speak eloquently, but if you are silent they do not stir the heart. They record the message, but you make plain what it means. They show us mysteries, but you reveal their hidden sense.[7]

As the Holy Spirit is the author of the scriptures, so the same Holy Spirit is the source of light and understanding.

While discussing the holy books, however, I would like to say a little more about the koan, about which I have spoken constantly in these pages. In dialogue with zen Buddhism and in the study of koan practice, can we Christians learn a new approach to our own scriptures?

The Zen Koan

I

Let me first admit that I hesitate to call the koan collections holy books, in view of the fact that they contain so little devotion. They are down-to-earth, existential, often humorous, often iconoclastic stories. But they do enshrine the Buddhist myth. They contain a series of very powerful symbols. And the person who solves the koan one by one (a process that takes many years or many decades) can fairly claim to have imbibed the essentials of Buddhism, to have seen into the essence of things, and to be living the life of the Buddha.

In all, there are some seventeen hundred koans contained in many collections, of which the most famous are the *Mumonkan* and the *Hekiganroku*.[8] Both of these were composed in China during the Sung dynasty (960–1279). Anyone who wants to go deeply into zen, following the way of the Rinzai sect, must systematically pass through the koans under the guidance of a master. Some of the koans relate real incidents in the lives of the shrewd Chinese masters, telling us what they said and how they treated their disciples. Others are just stories invented by the same masters to lead their disciples to enlightenment.

One begins zen practice by sitting in the lotus and counting the breathing. And when one has reached a certain facility in stilling the mind, one is given a koan that is taken into the depth of one's being, taken into one's belly. There one lives with it (if I were using Judaeo-Christian terms I would say that one "eats it," digests it) and identifies with the persons or things appearing in the story. To do this one must get away from all discursive reasoning and thinking in order to *become* the object. There must be no separation, no gap between myself and the object I contemplate. Put in other words, I must get beyond subject and object; I must lose myself, I must get away from every shred of dualistic thinking. In this way I die to self and become one with the object; I die to self and become one with the universe.

Ordinarily, the first koan which one receives is *mu*, about which I have already spoken in this book. In a certain sense *mu* is the first koan and the last. One can go deeper and deeper into *mu;* one can get growing insights into *mu*. The initial insight into *mu* is called *kensho* ("seeing into the essence of things"), but while passing through other koans, one can always return to *mu*. Indeed, all other enlightenments are no more than a deepening of this primary insight which is found through *mu*.

I have called it *mu,* but the complete version of the koan runs as follows: "A monk once asked Master Joshu, 'Has a dog the Buddha Nature or not?' Joshu said, *'Mu'* "[9] After receiving this koan, one takes *mu* into one's belly, sits with it, anguishes over it, lives it, becomes it. Then one goes to the master for the private interview known as *dokusan*.

"What is *mu?* " asks the master. "I am *mu,* " I answer. "Show me *mu,* " says the master. "You're looking at *mu,* " I answer. "What color is *mu?* " asks the master. "My color," I answer. "What shape is *mu?* " asks the master. "My shape," I answer. And in this way I demonstrate that I have really become *mu,* beyond all dualism, beyond all separation, beyond all possibility of illusion.

Other koans follow. There is, for example, the famous "sound of one hand clapping," to solve which I must become the hand. I thrust out my hand (just as Gutei held up his finger) and from my body language the master can immediately judge the degree of my enlightenment.

And these koans are surrounded by supplementary questions or commands. One of these is, "Stop the sound of the distant bell!" To one who is accustomed only to rational thinking this seems absurd, but the person who has mastered the art of identifying with the object will immediately exclaim: "Bong!" He or she becomes the bell and solves the koan.

The above are easy. But let me now cite some difficult koans.[10] The first is about the Zen Master Ba and runs as follows:

Master Ba was sick. The temple superintendent said: "Master Ba, how is your venerable health today?" Master Ba replied: "Sun-faced Buddha, moon-faced Buddha."[11]

In order to solve this koan one must first do a little practical exegesis to discover that sun-faced Buddha means a life of one day and one night, while moon-faced Buddha means a life of 18,000 years. And from this the rational answer is clear. Master Ba is saying: "A life of one day or a life of 18,000 years! What does it matter?" He has conquered the fear of death; he is totally liberated; he has gone beyond *samsara* to *nirvana*.

But an intellectual answer is useless in zen. One must not reason and think about the dying Master Ba. One must become Master Ba. From the belly one must spontaneously cry out, "sun-faced Buddha, moon-faced Buddha." In other words, one must existentially conquer the fear of death in an experience of joyful liberation.

But to conquer the fear of one's own death is not enough. Master Ba was not simply liberated from anxiety about his coming end. When he said, "sun-faced Buddha, moon-faced Buddha," he was liberated from life-and-death as such, liberated from the life and death of the universe, liberated from *samsara* and prepared to enter *nirvana*. And in becoming Master Ba I also attain to the same liberating enlightenment. This can be expressed in the word *mu* or in the great circle of nothingness which is the central symbol of zen.

Another famous koan is about Nansen and a cat, and it runs as follows:

> The monks of the eastern and western halls were quarrelling about a cat. The zen Master Nansen held up the cat by the tail and sternly said: "Monks, if anyone can say the right word, I will spare the cat. Otherwise I will kill it." No one answered; and Nansen, taking his sword, cut the cat in two. That same evening Nansen's favorite disciple, Joshu, returned to the temple. The monks told him the story; whereupon Joshu took off his sandals, put them on his head, and walked out of the room. "If he had been here," observed Nansen, "I would not have killed the cat."[12]

Here again, one solves the koan by a process of identification. One becomes the cat. That is to say, one gets cut in two; one gets killed; one dies. And note that this is a total death, because one who identifies with Nansen realizes that the great master kills not only the cat but also the monks, including himself. What an awful and total death! What a *mu* of nothingness!

But Nansen is a great and compassionate master. And zen tells us that his killing sword is a life-giving sword. In killing everybody he brings them to life. The monks who were previously quarreling are reborn to union. And Joshu acts this out by putting his sandals on his head and walking out of the room. He is a fool. Of course he is a fool, but he has transcended all the dualism of head and feet, hats and sandals, left and right, up and down. Totally liberated he has penetrated into the deepest caverns of *mu*.

II

From all this it will be amply clear that the aim of the koan is not to give information but to lead to enlightenment and to an existential conversion. And the disciple comes to this experience by body-reading the koan and identifying with it. Often this will be a painful experience because one must die—and dying is never easy—but through the anguish of death one rises to new life.

Yet the disciple does not pass through the koan alone; he needs the master. The master who is compassionate yet severe, the master who is highly enlightened but has not reached the goal, the master who is at once a Buddha and a dried shit-stick. To describe the encounter between master and disciple an old zen tradition uses three enigmatic symbols: heaven meeting earth as the lid meets the box; cutting off the flow of delusions; waves following waves.

Heaven meeting earth is the *yang* meeting the *yin* with great harmony and union as the lid fits the box. Cutting off the flow of delusions refers to the master's sharp and jolting cry that checks discursive thinking. Waves following waves indicates that the relationship flows on smoothly towards its goal.

But the basic question was: What can Christians learn from the koan? Can we read or meditate upon the Bible as the Buddhists meditate on the koan? Will we in this way come to a new understanding of our own scriptures? Will we in this way deepen our Christian enlightenment and our Christian commitment?

I believe that all these questions can be answered in the affirmative. Just as we enter into the scene in the "application of the senses" of St. Ignatius, so we can identify with the characters in the Bible after the fashion of the koan. And in this way we will find a powerful enlightenment. Let me give some examples of what I mean.

Take the story of the sin of David. Remember how the prophet Nathan pointed his finger at the king: "You are the man" (2 Sam. 12:7). This finger was indeed the killing sword. And David answered with the words: "I have sinned against the Lord" (2 Sam. 12.13). In this moment he died and rose to new life.

Now a Jew or a Christian who meditates on this text can identify with David. He or she must *become* David, must undergo that tremendous death, that tremendous conversion that issues in the humble and penitent cry: "I have sinned against the Lord." And can we not all utter these words? Can we not all identify with David? Because, even if we have not killed Uriah and stolen his wife, we have sinned in other ways and are capable of a betrayal like that of David. Once we come to the existential realization of our sinfulness through koan-like meditation on this passage, we can throw ourselves on the mercy of God, undergo a true conversion and rise to new life.

Again, as one meditates on the gospel one can identify with the various personalities who appear in its pages. Surely the wish of John is that one should identify with Thomas who knelt before Jesus and said: "My Lord and my God!" (John 20:28). This is the climax to which the whole gospel is leading: one must "die" with Thomas in order to rise to the new life of faith.

And I believe that in the Christian life one must finally identify with Jesus himself. Just as the aim of the Buddhist koan is to lead one to become the Buddha, so the aim of the Bible is to lead one to become Jesus, that is to say, to become a true child by grace as he is a child by nature. In other words we are back to the theme of the divinization of the human person, which is the great Christian enlightenment and which can be achieved (or, more properly, which is granted to us) when we become one with Jesus through love.

But in adapting koan practice to Christianity and the Bible, the principal problem is that of finding skilled masters. Western Christianity has not developed a dynamic of spiritual direction in which the master talks with the body and the disciple acts out the answer. Here is an area in which Christians have much to learn. And learn they will. Already some oriental Christian masters, steeped in their own tradition, are talking through the body and judging the degree of their disciples' enlightenment from their understanding of the

Bible. I believe that the oriental church of tomorrow will give birth to more such Christian masters who will lead their disciples to profound enlightenment and to identification with Jesus.

Hermeneutics Today

I

I have spoken about understanding the scriptures through commitment, through faith and through love, and I have spoken of the Christian belief that the author of the Bible is God himself. But the scriptures also have human authors, and it is the human dimension that has now come to the fore in the science of hermeneutics. Over the past century we have seen the rise of source criticism, of form criticism, of redaction criticism. We have come to recognize the literary genres of the various sacred books. And above all, studies in history, pre-history, archaeology, linguistics, textual criticism and the rest have thrown unprecedented light on the Bible. Scientifically speaking, we now know more about the Bible than at any time since it was written.

Naturally enough, the scholar who approaches the Bible in a scientific way asks himself or herself about the object of the inquiry. What is the object of the science of hermeneutics (the study of biblical meaning)? And to this question scholars at first answered confidently that they were searching for "the literal sense." This sounds reasonable and sound; but it was unsatisfactory because there was no agreement as to what the words "literal sense" meant. For a while scholars said that they were studying "the mind and intention of the human author as it was grasped by the people for whom he wrote." But this again was unsatisfactory for two reasons. First of all, it limited the meaning of the text to a certain time and place and public—without much relevance for later times. In other words, it restricted the universality of the biblical message. Secondly, and more importantly, it overlooked the fact (wisely stated by T. S. Eliot) that there is more in the poetry than the poet himself realizes. Yes, there is more in the Bible than the biblical authors realized. Just as literary criticism has extracted from Shakespeare's plays wonderful treasures that Shakespeare never dreamt of (think of the psychoanalytic interpretation of Hamlet), so biblical commentators can extract from the book of Job treasures of meaning that were not consciously in the mind of the author. Just as the plays of Shakespeare have profound meaning not just for sixteenth-century Englishmen but for peoples of all times, so the books of the Bible have meaning not just for the public to whom they were addressed but for men and women of all times.

And so in recent times there has been a shift from the author to the text. What are the words saying? What does the text mean? These are the pertinent questions, and here we are more likely to find "the literal sense."

Yet in asking these simple questions we run into extraordinary complexities, for we are confronted with the whole baffling mystery of human cognition. We are confronted with the awful question: What do I do when I know? And this is the question that has baffled philosophers from Plato to Kant and from Aristotle to Russell. I have dealt with it in my first chapter. Here let me only repeat that *all knowledge is creative*. The external object is no more than the data of consciousness. From this data we create our world of meaning. And if this is true of any act of cognition, how much more true of artistic and literary criticism. The work of art only comes to life when there is a mind to understand it; the musical score only comes to life when there is a pianist to perform it; Hamlet only comes to life when a skilled actor plays the role of the Prince of Denmark. The skilled pianist and the talented actor are highly creative, highly individualistic interpreters. And in the same way the authentic biblical interpreter is a highly creative person. Of course he must be faithful to the text (just as the pianist must be faithful to the score) but he is also creating something new. And if it is difficult to understand how this can be so, that is because it is difficult to understand what knowing is—human understanding and creativity are indeed difficult to understand. Here we are faced with the mystery of the human spirit.

Now all that I have said will be radically denied by the naive realist. He or she thinks that the Bible is "out there" to be looked at. He or she will contend that there can be a really "objective" understanding of the Bible, that there could be a definitive once-for-all commentary, and that the person who knows this commentary is right and the person who does not know it is wrong.[13] Yet, alas, this is a way of thinking that no sane philosopher would accept today. Because just as the physicist is involved with the subatomic world he studies, so the interpreter is involved with the text he interprets. Such naive objectivity is a dream that has long since passed away.

And so it is more real to look on literary and artistic criticism not as an interpretation of something "out there," but as a dialogue between the reader and the book, a dialogue in which something new and beautiful is created through the dynamism of the human mind. And if this is true of all literature, it is equally true of the Bible. One dialogues with the text. To do this authentically, it is true, one must understand the literary genres and one should be familiar with form criticism, but these simply provide the data upon which one builds so as to understand and judge creatively.

In all that I have said here I have been treating the scriptures as human books and as classics of literature; and I have been saying that one who looks for the literal sense must approach them as one would approach the plays of Shakespeare or the music of Beethoven or the history of Thucydides. But now let me move on to the fact that the Bible is also a religious book.

II

Christian scholars, needless to say, have not forgotten that the Bible is a religious book and that God is its author. And, in consequence, they have claimed that it contains a "fuller sense" or *sensus plenior* that goes far beyond the literal sense. This fuller sense, they have maintained, was not in the conscious mind of the author and, perhaps, not even in the text itself. But it was intended by God who is the ultimate author.

This, again, sounds reasonable, but it bristles with problems, the chief of which is that it frequently makes God into a *deus ex machina* who descends from the clouds and has little connection with the author or the text. Surely this is an embarrassing situation. It seems to me that the pertinent and challenging question is the following: Can I find this fuller sense *in the text*?

And my contention is that it is possible to do so. My contention is that we get to this *sensus plenior* not through scholarship but through love. Not just any kind of love but the love we call religious because it is unrestricted, because it goes on and on and on, because it is bound up with total commitment. This is the love that Nichiren had for the Lotus Sutra; this is the love that Augustine and Jerome had for the Bible. It may express itself in the body-reading I have described, or in the Ignatian application of the senses, or in the relishing and savoring of the words, or in eating the sweet-as-honey scroll, or in the koan-like identification with the characters of the Bible. Yes, all these ways of meditation, properly understood, are expressions of unrestricted love and of total commitment. And they all lead to profound wisdom (that *sapientia* of which the Christian tradition delicately speaks) and they all call down the Holy Spirit, who comes to dwell within us and to teach us by his gentle whisperings and his delicate stirrings.

In short, there are two kinds of knowledge: one that comes from scholarship and another that comes from love. And far from being imcompatible, they complement one another. They fit together like heaven and earth, like the lid and the box, like the head and the belly, like the *yin* and the *yang*.

And there is one more important point. I have talked about love. Now I do not mean just the love of the individual but also, and more importantly, the love of the community. Throughout the world millions of Christians have lovingly read, or listened to, the word of God in the liturgy, in prayer groups, in classrooms, in monasteries. Millions of Christians have savored and relished the sacred words in quiet, contemplative prayer. And all this loving contemplation has led to an ongoing wisdom and insight into the mysteries of the word. Such was the doctrine of the Second Vatican Council, which writes as follows:

> For there is a growth in the understanding of the realities and the words that have been handed down. This happens through the contemplation and study made by believers, who treasure these things in their hearts (cf. Luke 2:19, 51), through the intimate understanding of spiritual things they experience, and through the preaching of those who have received through episcopal succession the sure gift of truth. For, as the centuries succeed one another, the Church constantly moves forward toward the fullness of divine truth until the words of God reach their complete fulfillment in her.[14]

This is a remarkable passage. Clearly it rejects naive realism and affirms forcefully the evolutionary character of scriptural exegesis. And it beautifully points to the contemplative prayer of Mary who wonderingly tasted and savored the memory of the great events to which she had been exposed: "But Mary kept all these things, pondering them in her heart" (Luke 2:19). Following the example of Mary, the Christian community savors the scriptures and engenders a growth that will continue until the parousia.

So now we know that the interpretation of the scriptures will never come to an end. We will never have the definitive commentary. As long as the human race continues, new treasures will be found in the scriptures through the contemplative love of the people of God.

And of course this has an exciting corollary for those of us who live in Asia. It means that, as Christianity puts down roots, there will be a new, Asian interpretation of the scriptures. This new hermeneutic will not, of course, neglect what has been done in the West, but it will give the church new insights; it will throw new light on old truths. And, indeed, something like this is already happening in India and Japan where commentators on the scriptures are opening up new vistas which the West never saw. Who can guess what the future will hold?

III

And now we must ask if it is possible to find a method that will unite the various approaches to the scriptures. Is it possible to find a method that will harmoniously bring together the scholarly and the religious?

I believe it is. I believe we can bring these various strands together by fidelity to the transcendental precepts that tell us to be attentive, intelligent, reasonable, responsible and loving.

Be attentive! In obedience to this we learn all we can about the historical, geographical and archaeological background to the Bible. Above all, we are attentive to the words of the text and we are sensitive to the literary genre. All this means hard work. It may mean blood and tears and sweat and toil, but anyone who wants to understand the scriptures in depth cannot neglect it.

And from this attentiveness and questioning there will come insight. Here we are creative and come to an *understanding* of the text. Furthermore, we will sift out our insights and make objective statements about what is really said in the text and what its true meaning is. We will also make value judgments about the worth of the Bible. And in this way we will come to discover the great literary and artistic treasures of Hebrew literature, just as a Shakespearean critic discovers the wonders of the plays of Shakespeare.

But if we have faith, we will not stop here. For we will love the text and be committed to it, and this love will carry us beyond the literal sense to the fuller sense or *sensus plenior*. Now we will meditate on the great scenes of scripture, repeating the words and relishing them. Like Mary, we will turn these things over in our hearts with wonder. We will eat the scroll; we will identify with the characters. Through love we will come to a greater and greater understanding of the realities outlined in the text.

And then, as our love grows, it becomes a spiritual passion, a falling in love with the Word who draws us beyond words and phrases into the cloud of unknowing. Now we are no longer preoccupied with the mind of the author nor even with the words of the text, but with the great reality towards which the words point, the great reality that cannot be understood by the discursive intellect, the great reality which cannot be known by reason but only by love, the great reality that is Yahweh himself. Buddhism truly says that words and letters are like a finger pointing to the moon, and we discover that this is true even of the words of the Bible. They point the way to God and are, so to speak, the jumping-off ground. But when I attain to God through love, I can abandon all words and letters, even the words and letters of the Bible.

In this way, the contemplative reading of the Bible is a way to mysticism. It is a dialogue. But now rather than comparing it to a dialogue with the text of Shakespeare, I would prefer to compare it to the loving dialogue between the bridegroom and the bride. This is the very image used by the Second Vatican Council when it writes that "God, who spoke of old, uninterruptedly converses with the Bride of His beloved Son; and the Holy Spirit, through whom the living voice of the gospel resounds in the Church, and through her, in the world, leads unto all truth those who believe and makes the word of Christ dwell abundantly in them (cf. Col. 3:16)."[15]

IV

And as my dialogue with the scriptures develops into a passionate love affair, far from despising the scientific knowledge of the scholars I feel a desire to learn all the details about the Word Incarnate. I come to love Jesus of Nazareth so much that I desire to go to Jerusalem to see with my own eyes the land in which Jesus lived and taught. In this connection St. Ignatius tells a humorous story about himself. Just after leaving Jerusalem he realized with a shock that he had forgotten the exact direction in which the footprints of Jesus were pointing on the Mount of Olives. So, bribing the Turkish guide with a knife, he went back to examine the spot. Needless to say, these "footprints" were not authentic. My point is that great mystical love inspired him to seek factual knowledge.

Interpreting the Bible

I

All the great religions have their teachers or theologians or masters, who comment on the holy books profoundly and creatively. The zen master gives his homily or *teisho* by commenting on some Buddhist text or on some koan, and often these *teisho* are preserved in books for subsequent generations. And in the same way Christianity has always had its enlightened commentators from the time of Origen and Augustine and Jerome.

And our age needs its commentators too. We need men and women who are steeped in the sacred text and who will, at the same time, speak to contemporary problems. What qualities, then, do we expect to find in a great contemporary commentator? I would suggest three qualities.

First, I would say that the great commentator is a person with a certain scholarly knowledge of the Bible. He is familiar with the literary genres; he knows the historical and geographical background; he is familiar with biblical studies, both modern and ancient. And so his comments are scholarly.

Second, he is a great artist. He feels deeply the biblical message and has a delicate sympathy with the text. He is creative. As a great pianist interprets the nocturnes of Chopin, so he interprets the Bible faithfully yet with new insight. And so his comments are inspiring. Third, he is a great mystic. He has profound faith in, and love for, the Bible. He has meditated on the text for many years; he has tasted and eaten the scroll. And a passionately spiritual love for the Bible has carried him beyond the words of the text to a wordless silence and to a direct contact with the great reality towards which the words point. This means that he frequently knows more about these realities than the human authors of the Bible. He will speak powerfully about Genesis because, like Moses, he has met Yahweh, the Lord of Heaven and Earth, and has spoken to him face to face, as a man might speak with his friend. He can make his own the words of Jesus: "Truly, truly, I say to you, we speak of what we know, and bear witness to what we have seen . . ." (John 3:11).

Such biblical commentators were the church fathers, Aquinas, St. John of the Cross, Meister Eckhart, Johannes Tauler and a host of others. The mystics quote passage after passage of the Bible, and naive realists pooh-pooh their exegesis. But more thoughtful people realize that these mystics really knew the Bible, and that one way to understand the sacred books is to read the great classics of the mystical life.

But can we point to one commentator and say that he was the greatest? Is there one who towers over all the others?

I believe there is one such. The Jesus of Nazareth who appears in the pages of the four gospels is the greatest biblical commentator. Remember how the Lucan Jesus expounds to the two disciples going to Emmaus all that was written about him in the law of Moses and the prophets and the psalms. Think of the powerful Johannine portrait of a Jesus who has read the scriptures again and again and has found himself therein. In the fourth gospel, the great conflict between Jesus and his adversaries centers around the interpretation of the scriptures, and Jesus hurls at them those striking words: "If you believed Moses, you would believe me, for he wrote of me" (John 5:46). Jesus was, in effect, telling his adversaries that if they knew their own scriptures they would accept him: "You search the scriptures, because you think that in them you have eternal life; and it is they that bear witness to me . . ." (John 5:39).

And Jesus had this extraordinary knowledge of the scriptures because he had a unique and extraordinary knowledge of the reality toward which they point. He alone knew the Father: "No one has ever seen God; the only Son, who is in the bosom of the Father, he has made him known" (John 1:18). And the person who, identified with Jesus, knows the Father will truly understand the scriptures and will expound them forcefully to contemporary people.

NOTES

1. Gandhi read and reread the *Bhagavad Gita.* Strictly speaking the *Gita* is not a Hindu scripture, but it has always been revered as a holy book.
2. The Buddhist scriptures are divided into three main sections which are called *pitakas* or baskets. The *Sutra-pitaka* contains the scriptures that are said to have been taught by the Buddha himself, though in fact it contains many later additions. The *Vinaya-pitaka* is a collection of ethical rules. The *Abhidharma-pitaka* contains discussions on the above two. Apart from Tibetans, most Mahayana Buddhists use the Chinese version.
3. In Japanese, *Hoke-kyo;* Sanskrit, *Saddharma-pundarika-sutra.* This sutra is said to have been translated from Sanskrit into Chinese six times, but three of these translations were already lost by the year 730.
4. For an excellent description of the body-reading of the koan and the Bible see Kakichi Kadowaki, *Zen and the Bible* (London: Routledge and Kegan Paul, 1979).
5. *De Imitatione Christi,* Bk. 4, c. 11.
6. "Dogmatic Constitution on Divine Revelation," c.6. The notion that the church venerates scripture as she venerates the Body of the Lord is found in the fathers of the church, particularly in St. Jerome and St. Augustine. See Augustine Bea, *The Word of God and Mankind* (Chicago: Herald Press, 1967), p. 267.
7. *De Imitatione Christi,* Bk. 3, c. 2.
8. The *Mumonkan* is a one-fascicle collection of forty-eight koan and was compiled by Mumon Ekai. The *Hekiganroku* is a ten-fascicle collection containing one hundred koan.
9. *Mumonkan* 1.
10. Koans are classified into various groups among which are the *nanto* or difficult-to-pass koan. For a description of the various koan groupings see Isshū Miura and Ruth Fuller Sasaki, *Zen Dust* (Kyoto: First Zen Society, 1966).
11. *Hekiganroku* 3.
12. Ibid., 63.
13. Sandra Schneiders quotes an eminent biblical scholar who in the 1950s stated that "if all scholars were perfectly objective, entire unanimity should be theoretically possible in exegesis itself; for the meaning of the Bible has been determined by its authors, not by its interpreters." See Sandra M. Schneiders, "Faith, Hermeneutics, and the Literal Sense of Scripture," *Theological Studies,* December 1978.
14. "Dogmatic Constitution on Divine Revelation," c. 2.
15. Ibid.

6

Transformation of Feeling

O VER THE PAST few decades, the Western world has come to appreciate in an unprecedented manner the role of feeling in human life. This development owes much to Freud and the psychoanalysts, who pointed out that most people are moved and motivated less by reason than by the deep subliminal feelings that lie at the depth of the unconscious mind. This insight brought about great changes, including a sexual revolution that made people aware of their sexuality as never before. This was followed by an affective revolution that made us aware of our affectivity—our joys and our fears, our hopes and our frustrations, our cheerfulness and our depression, our tenderness and our anger. And then came what I might call the mystical revolution when people, particularly young people, turning their eyes longingly towards the temples of Kyoto, the ashrams of Delhi and the topless towers of Shangri-La, felt the subtle fascination of zen and yoga and lamaism. Then there arose interest in Western mysticism and in charismatic experiences such as speaking in tongues, dancing, prophesying and healing. And in all this it became clear, clear, clear that Western culture had been suffering from too much *yang*, too much "head," too much of the masculine; what it needed was a good dose of *yin*, of the "belly," of the feminine.

And so, feeling came to occupy the center of the picture—with all kinds of practical consequences. Now we are told to accept our feelings, to value them, to live them. There is no more talk of "mere feelings" or "mere emotion." No, we are told to follow our instincts, to accept our femininity, to listen to our inner stirrings, to record our dreams. We are warned not to repress feelings by pushing them into the unconscious; for if we do that, they will certainly take revenge by exploding in our face or by causing some nauseating psychosomatic illness. Or they will break out in overeating, or in grasping for power or money, or in excessive severity towards ourselves and others. Indeed, we now know, repressed feelings may cleverly masquerade as virtues; we may think that we are very pious and holy people when, in fact, we are frustrated, angry and deprived. Such is the beautiful, yet devastating role of feeling in human life.

And if the discovery of feeling has brought much joy, it has also brought much suffering. For one thing, people are now asking questions they never asked before—about their sexual identity, about their relationship with father and mother, about their hidden motivation in the great choices of life. And the answer to these questions often shocks them profoundly. Again, there is the problem of how to fulfill these stark emotional needs, and of how to cope with the feelings that have been unleashed. It is clear (as, again, Freud and the psychoanalysts pointed out) that we cannot always control feelings by strength of will, as the old books said. "I will" and "I will not" can be counter-productive in the realm of feeling. No amount of willing controls the superego; no amount of willing overcomes alcoholism or acute anxiety or homosexuality. If we indulge in too much will, we may find that the very thing we do not want to do is the thing we end up doing.

The Way of Affectivity

I

Now in the midst of all these stormy revolutions people, naturally enough, looked for guidance to traditional religion with the questions: "What are Buddhism and Christianity saying about feeling? Are they teaching us to cope with the affective tempest that has engulfed us? Are they showing us the way to that refinement of feeling to which we aspire? Are they leading us to that apex of human affectivity which we call mysticism?"

And many who asked these questions were sadly disappointed. It seemed to them that both Buddhism and Christianity, far from educating human feeling, had despised and crushed it. And so they felt a certain anger and rebellion, analogous to the anger that adolescents experience against their parents. Such righteous indignation, of course, is not new. I am reminded of a zen story about a pious old woman who built a hermitage for a monk and for years brought him his food. One day she decided that she would test him. So she sent her pretty niece to bring his food, telling her to embrace him and bring back news of how he reacted. The girl duly embraced the holy man, who roughly pushed her away with the words: "Sap does not rise in a withered tree!" The niece told this to the woman, who immediately stormed up to the hermitage. "For years I have been looking after a block of wood," she cried. Then she drove the monk away and burned the hermitage.

The woman felt that zen had turned the monk into a dehumanized block of wood, and a similar feeling of resentment has arisen in many modern Christians when they reflect on how seminaries and novitiates have crushed tenderness and compassion and human feeling. For Christians realize instinctively that this should not be so, in view of the tenderness of Jesus himself. Think of the Jesus who defended Mary when she anointed his feet with the costly ointment of pure nard. This is the Jesus who wept over Jerusalem, the Jesus who indignantly drove the money-changers from the temple. This is the Jesus on whose breast the beloved disciple tenderly laid his head. This is the Jesus who sweated blood in Gethsemane. What depth of feeling we see in the founder of Christianity!

If, then, we are to be faithful to Jesus of Nazareth and to the contemporary world, we must purify and update our religious practice in such a way that it will lead to an affective conversion—an affective conversion, thanks to which feeling will flower and flourish and assume its rightful place in the Christian life. Such a conversion is eminently possible. For, rightfully understood, Christian prayer leads to a wonderful refinement of human feeling, to the vivification of the interior senses, to a transformation and transfiguration of affectivity and sexuality. This is what I call an affective conversion. Let me now describe how this comes about.

II

Traditional Christianity has always encouraged what was called "intimacy with God" or "holy familiarity with God" or "familiarity with Jesus and Mary." This is a style of prayer in which one brings to the Lord one's joys and fears and anxieties. One speaks spontaneously to Jesus or to Mary or to the Father about one's temptations, about one's desolation, about one's anxieties and fears, about one's sexuality, about one's successes and failures, about one's dreams. In a simple way, one brings one's total self before the Lord and speaks to him as to a loving friend who sympathizes and understands. If feelings of anger or disgust arise in the mind and heart, one expresses them to the Lord freely and without inhibition. One may protest angrily to God: "Why have you done this to me? Why have you let this happen?" Or one may break out in spontaneous praise or thanksgiving or adoration, as one reflects on the good and beautiful things that have happened in one's life and in the world. Or one may make prayers of petition for oneself or one's loved ones. And in this way, one grows in intimacy with God, praying in the manner of the psalmist, or of Job, or of Jesus himself.

Such has been, and still is, the prayer of millions of Catholic Christians who quietly kneel or sit before the Blessed Sacrament in churches throughout the world, looking towards Jesus, the beautiful mirror in which they see the reflection of themselves and their sufferings. In this prayer nothing is too trivial or ugly to be brought out. No feelings are rammed down into the unconscious, there to fester and smolder and cause problems. On the contrary, all is brought to the light, and a wonderful self-acceptance is effected. Of course I see ugly as well beautiful things within myself, but God is compassionate and loving. He wants me to be compassionate towards myself as he is compassionate, to love myself as he loves me. So the very sight of my ugly dimension can bring great joy. Moreover, as can be seen, there are no distractions in this prayer, for the distractions are the

114

very raw material and content. Only one must remain with God. And this is a prayer practiced both by simple beginners and by consummate mystics.

And, of course, there are other forms of affective prayer. I have already pointed out how some people use the feelings and imagination in reading the scriptures, how they taste and relish and savor and eat the sacred books. I have pointed out how one can repeat the Jesus prayer with loving devotion. I have pointed out how, with Ignatius, one can apply the senses to scenes of the gospel. Let me again quote Ignatius whose method "consists in seeing in imagination the persons, and in contemplating and meditating in detail the circumstances in which they are, and in drawing fruit . . . ."[1] After *seeing*, one *hears*, and in the third point, one is invited "to *smell* the infinite fragrance, and *taste* the infinite sweetness of the divinity"; and later one is asked to *touch* and to *embrace* and to *kiss* the place where the persons stand or are seated.

Here Ignatius is obviously leading to a wonderful refinement of the senses. From seeing and hearing (which a beginner can do) he leads to the more interior and more refined senses of smell and taste and touch. Elsewhere the same Ignatius sets great store by tears. And, interestingly enough, there are three kinds of tears: There are exterior tears that we all shed in time of grief or frustration; there are those torrents of tears that stream down the face when the mind and heart are filled with deep, deep peace and even with joy; and then there are those other tears that pour forth abundantly and powerfully from the inner eyes, even when the outer eyes are dry.[2]

Again, affectivity is the key to Ignatian discernment. Ignatius wants us to be aware of those deep, subliminal feelings that we ordinarily ignore. I doubt, though, if he would have joined the happy chorus that cries: "Trust your instincts!" He was more subtle. He knew full well that some spiritual instincts are trustworthy and will lead to self-realization, but others will lead to self-destruction. Indeed, some feelings that seem pious and holy are, in fact, inspired by one who disguises himself as an angel of light. And we must discern. We must, above all, watch for that "consolation without previous cause" that wells up from the substance of the soul and the core of our being. For this is a very, very precious feeling. We must watch the beginning, middle and end of the interior stirrings to see if all is leading towards good. We must watch for those delicate, mystical feelings that gently enter our hearts like the drop of water falling on a sponge. Such feelings we must relish and cultivate.

III

St. John of the Cross, great poet that he is, talks richly about inebriation with wine and intoxication with love. If this language shocks and embarrasses good people, let them recall that he is talking about the interior senses that have their roots deep down in the human psyche. The Holy Spirit, who dwells in the center of the soul, is like lamps of fire that transform and transfigure those unruly and disorderly senses that were dark and blind because of original sin. Now they are renewed so that they give warmth and light to the Beloved who dwells within. Here are the saint's words:

> O Lamps of fire
> In whose splendors
> The deep caverns of feeling,
> Once obscure and blind,
> Now give forth, so rarely, so exquisitely,
> Both warmth and light to their Beloved.[3]

When one reflects that the cave is a symbol of the unconscious, one can understand that the purification of these "deep caverns of feeling" is profound indeed.

But to understand the nature of this transformation it is necessary to recall that earlier chapter where I spoke of a seeing that is not seeing, a hearing that is not hearing, a breathing that is not breathing. Now we have the same pattern. As there is an exterior touch, so there is an interior touch; as there is an exterior inebriation, so there is an interior inebriation; as there are exterior tears, so there are interior tears; as there is an exterior eros, so there is an interior eros; as there is an exterior sexuality, so there is an interior sexuality. But (and this is important) the interior senses are not built on rejection of the exterior. No, the exterior senses have been deepened, transformed, transfigured.

But this transformation does not take place without struggle or suffering. Indeed, there seems to be a psychological law that a period or periods of emptiness and dryness are necessary prior to the emergence of the new level of feeling that we call interior, or mystical, affectivity. Yes, the field must lie fallow before the new harvest can be gathered. The exterior senses must fast in order that the interior senses may come to life. The grain of wheat, falling into the ground, must die in order to bring forth much fruit.

And so the mystics talk about the desert experience. This may take the form of a long period—sometimes years—of interior darkness and aridity. But more often, I believe, it follows the *yin-yang* cycle of light-darkness-light-darkness-light. In either case there can be tempestuous periods of fear and anguish, of sexual upheaval, of scrupulosity, of near despair. There can be times of real human weakness when the mystic falls headlong in the mud. There may also be exterior sufferings such as failure, rejection or sickness. But the wise director is always gentle, always compassionate, always encouraging, because he knows that these periods of darkness are of inestimable value and that transformation is taking place.

Indeed St. John of the Cross waxes eloquent about the benefits of the dark night, as he sings:

> O guiding night
> O night more lovely than the dawn!
> O night that has united
> The Lover with His beloved,
> Transforming the beloved in her Lover.[4]

The poet sees that this night is touching the very roots of the personality which are not affected by "I will" and "I will not." The dark night is penetrating to even deeper layers of the psyche than psychoanalysis. And, like psychoanalysis, it is healing anxieties, neuroses, sexual problems, addictions of all kinds. It is effecting an astonishing inner freedom.

The old authors claimed that the tempest is unavoidable. No one acquires virtue without struggle. No one possesses courage who has not felt fear; no one possesses peace who has not felt conflict; no one possesses chastity who has not felt inordinate sexuality; no one can say he or she loves who has not been tempted to hate; no one knows strength who has not felt weakness. Perhaps this is one more example of the *yin* and the *yang*—only by coming to the verge of despair can one swing back to the pinnacle of hope.

IV

And so the dark night is a necessary part of the transformation of affectivity, and St. John of the Cross is anxious to lead people into it. He does so in two ways.

The first way is that of personal effort. One strives, for love of Christ, to renounce anything that may be an obstacle to chaste and perfect love. It should be noted, however, that in his program of asceticism (and a terrible program it is) the saint never rejects any of God's created things. He speaks of "non-use." When I fast, I do not say that food is bad. I simply do not use it. And in the same way, there can be a fasting of the senses and of the mind; this is outlined powerfully in *The Ascent of Mount Carmel*.

The second way is that of *wu-wei* or letting things happen. Here I let God lead me into the night; I let God do his work; I let God love me; I do not hinder the process that is taking place. In other words, I do not fight against the night but sit quietly in the darkness. This, again, is powerfully described in *The Dark Night*.

About these periods of darkness, however, a couple of warnings must be made.

The first is this. Quite often, good and pious people have thought they were in the dark night when, in fact, they were at an earlier stage of growth; they were undergoing the depression that inevitably settles on persons who have crushed their affectivity. They have thought that they should starve their exterior senses and abandon affective prayer precisely when they should have aroused their affectivity, calling out to God in joy or love or anger or dismay. And this has been disastrous. It is one of the consequences of a premature and superficial reading of mystical literature. One should pray with the affections as long as one is able to do so. One should never enter the dark night until one is drawn therein.

Again, unskilled directors (and this was a problem in the old novitiates) have sometimes applied the ascetical rules of the dark night to tender beginners. They have encouraged mere novices to desire suffering and embrace humiliation. This again has been disastrous. For while it is true that in the mystical life a time comes when, like Paul, one can glory in the cross of Our Lord Jesus Christ, this time cannot be forced. "Do not awaken love before its time." St. John of the Cross never made such a mistake. He says explicitly that he is writing for a few contemplatives of his own order; he had no intention of writing a best-seller.

But let me return to the nights. Do they ever end? I do not think so. In this mortal life there will always be light and darkness, as there is *yin* and *yang*. But the mystics do love to celebrate the passage from darkness to light. They hear ringing in their ears the words of the Lord:

> Arise, my love, my fair one,
>   and come away;
> for lo, the winter is past,
>   the rain is over and gone. [Cant. 2:10,11]

Yes, the winter is past. I am loved; I am chosen; I am the beautiful one, the fair one. This is the time of joy and light. And yet, in a sense, it is not light. It is not that the darkness has given way to light, but rather that I have come to love the darkness. Night has not gone, but the *oppressive night* has become the *tranquil night*. God was not absent; he was present all the time but I did not recognize him. Whereas I was blind, now I see. Put in other terms, mystical experience is an acquired taste. At first it is bitter to the palate; but eventually one comes to love what was formerly oppressive.

V

My point has been that authentic Christian prayer does not destroy human affectivity but transforms it. It spiritualizes matter and divinizes the human person. Let us remember that it is not just the spirit that is divinized through the grace of Christ but also the body and the senses. And all this is a preparation for that resurrection of which the Risen Jesus is the model and exemplar.

But let me end with a word of caution. The transformation of the senses is never completed in this life. Human nature is always weak. Neuroses and fears and storms and upheavals can remain until death. Indeed, temptations become more subtle and dangerous as matter is progressively spiritualized and refined. Human life, said the old authors, is a warfare. And that brings us back to the never-to-be-forgotten shit-stick of Unmon. "Therefore let anyone who thinks that he stands take heed lest he fall," said Paul (1 Cor. 10:12). And this applies to the most advanced mystic.

Eros and Agape

I

From what has been said it will be clear that in the Christian life the transformation of the senses is effected through love—through the ongoing, unrestricted, unconditional love we call *agape*. This is the love of which Paul says that it "bears all things, believes all things, hopes all things, endures all things . . . love never ends" (1 Cor. 13:7, 8). This is the love than which there is no greater because it makes one lay down one's life for one's friends. This is the love the medievals called "chaste and perfect" because it is liberated from all self-centered clinging. This is the love which is necessarily extreme. All other virtues, says Thomas Aquinas, following Aristotle, are found in the golden mean; but we cannot love too much.

And Christian perfection consists in this agape love. Such was the conclusion of medieval theology, after many controversies about the value of contemplation and poverty and chastity and the other virtues. And later theologians went a step further with the thesis that not only Christian perfection but also Christian mysticism consists in agape. Moreover, many of them (with whom I am in complete agreement) maintained that this mystical love, far from being a gift of the privileged few, is a normal development of the Christian life. In baptism one receives the Holy Spirit and one grows to mysticism through prayer and through the sacraments.

The problem confronting us now, however, is: What is the nature of this God-given love which we call agape? And what is its relationship to the affective life which we have been discussing? Since, clearly enough, it is not an ethereal spiritual power but a deeply human love that is always incarnate in a heart of flesh, one would expect it to develop and grow through the ordinary process of living. And I believe that this is so.

Speaking of the development of the *anima* (or feminine principle in man) Jung gives us four symbols that are very helpful here. They are Eve, Helen, Mary and Sophia.[5] Eve stands for biological love; Helen of Troy, for romantic love; the Virgin Mary, for devotional love; Sophia, for mystical love. Here it is interesting to note that Jung clearly distinguishes between religious love represented by Sophia and erotic love represented by Helen. He held that the religious instinct was different from the sexual instinct, and this was one of the points on which he broke with Freud.

In the practical working out of these four symbols he was probably thinking in terms of four levels of consciousness (for just as there are levels of awareness, so there can be levels of love), for he intimates that at our present stage of evolution few arrive at the sapiential level of mysticsm. However, he tosses the whole thing out provocatively without development, so perhaps I will be permitted to develop these symbols in my own way.

It seems to me that in the Christian life Sophia is present from the beginning—or, more correctly, is present from the time of baptism. It is the love that is "poured out into our hearts by the Holy Spirit which has been given to us" (Rom. 5:5). And it can co-exist with, and vivify, the biological love symbolized by Eve as well as the romantic love symbolized by Helen.

The union of Eve and Sophia is found clearly in the Song of Songs which eloquently expresses both eros and agape. I need hardly say here that this beautiful canticle has been a source of embarrassment to many pious Christians who have been alarmed by its overt eroticism. Let them be at ease. In certain circumstances, cannot agape be united with eros? What makes agape to be agape is not its purely spiritual qualities but the fact that it is unconditional, unrestricted, total and ongoing. And such is the love of the Song of Songs. Surely there is a totality and an unrestrictedness in the claim that "love is strong as death"; and in the words:

> Many waters cannot quench love
> neither can floods drown it.
> If a man offered for love
> all the wealth of his house,
> it would be utterly scorned. [Cant. 8:7]

These words can stand confidently beside the Pauline canticle of love in First Corinthians. They illustrate my point that agape, far from killing or destroying sexuality and eroticism, transforms and transfigures them.

And the same holds true for the second symbol, which is that of Helen. Since the language of romantic love, which she represents, appears constantly in the mystics, allow me to treat of it in more detail.

II

One of the most significant events in the affective development in the West was the rise of the so-called courtly love, which appeared quite suddenly at the end of the eleventh century in southern France and is associated with the poets known as troubadours. C. S. Lewis, in a well-known book, claims that these poets "effected a change which has left no corner of our ethics, our imagination, or our daily life untouched. . . . Compared with this revolution the Renaissance is a mere ripple on the surface of literature."[6] And yet C. S. Lewis is wary of this courtly love and laments that "its characteristics may be enumerated as Humility, Courtesy, Adultery, and the religion of love."[7] He maintains that as this great movement had a beginning (it was unknown in the Greco-Roman world), so it will have an end.

And while C. S. Lewis was reflecting negatively on courtly love and its development, other contemporary writers were describing, not without melodrama, the dire conflict between eros and agape. Eros, they maintained, stands for the dark and deathly forces of Greek and Roman paganism, whereas agape stands for the gentle power of Christian love. Eros is the wildly physical, material and seductive harlot, whereas agape is the inspiring and beautiful woman of God.[8]

But over against this was the undeniable fact that courtly love and eros had inspired much of the poetry and art of the Christian world— it had its influence on Dante, on Chaucer, on Shakespeare. It influenced St. Francis of Assisi, who called himself "God's trouba- dour." It influenced the whole chivalrous devotion to the Virgin Mary that flourished in the Middle Ages and that we see exemplified in an Ignatius who spends a vigil of arms before the statue of Mary after his conversion. And, of course, the language of courtly love fills the pages of the Spanish mystics. Listen to St. John of the Cross:

> Upon my flowering breast
> which I kept wholly for him alone,
> There he lay sleeping,
> And I caressing him
> There in a breeze from the fanning cedars.[9]

If courtly love was an anti-Christian invasion from the so-called pagan world, how explain its influence on poets and mystics?

Some writers have hinted that the mystics used the language of courtly love inadvertently, without knowing its source. But this is unlikely. It seems to me more probable that they saw a core of goodness in courtly love; they knew it could be baptized and transformed. I believe that when Francis called himself God's troubadour, he meant that he was head-over-heels in love with God in much the same way as the troubadour was head-over-heels in love with his chosen lady. But the love of Francis was transformed and transfigured and purified. Moreover, it was transformed not by becoming "more spiritual" but by becoming unconditional, unrestricted and ongoing, with God as its object. Again, in the stanza I have quoted, St. John of the Cross is speaking about agape in terms of eros. He, too, understands that eros can be transformed and transfigured and that it can co-exist with the most powerful agape.

For the fact is that talk about the conflict between eros and agape is a false statement of an important problem. From what I have said it should be clear that agape does not reject eros but transforms it, just as it transforms the seeing and the hearing and the touching and the breathing and all the senses. It is true, of course, that this transformation does not take place without that struggle which I have called the dark night. But it is false to think of eros and agape as implacable enemies.

To this let me add another reflection. Some theologians who have written on this subject have attacked courtly love because it is nonbiblical. C. S. Lewis, while maintaining that the source of courtly love is unclear, is adamant in affirming that nothing like courtly love is found in the Bible. Jung himself may have seen this, because while Eve, Mary and Sophia are biblical figures, Helen steps out of the pages of the *Iliad*.

But does the fact that something is nonbiblical make it the enemy of Christianity? Does the fact that something is nonbiblical make it unacceptable to Christians? I do not think so. For Christianity has always found itself capable of dialogue with the non-Christian world, as it is in dialogue with Hinduism and Buddhism today. And I myself believe that courtly love, for all its defects, is basically a very human sentiment that had to arise in the affective evolution of the human race. I believe we must thank the great poets and mystics who saw its beauty and, learning from the troubadours, transformed this kind of affectivity and led it to agape.

If you ask me, then, why the mystics use the language of eros to explain the experience of agape, I would suggest three reasons. The first is that mystical experience cannot be expressed in ordinary language and so the mystics either say nothing or have recourse to symbolism. Living in that culture and that literary environment it was altogether natural that they should take their symbolism from courtly love. Second, the language of eros is unrestricted and unconditional—and this fits the unconditional nature of agape; one needs very extreme language to talk about the all-consuming love of God that comes to fill the heart in mysticism. Third, I believe that an element of eros, of a transformed and transfigured eros, is usually present in the mystical experience side by side with agape, since divine love destroys or annihilates nothing in the human psyche.

III

I have tried to say that agape is completely compatible with Eve and Helen. In the practical order this means that a married person can be an advanced mystic and that his or her mystical love will flow into, and strengthen, his or her sexual and erotic life, as well as his or her affective love for family and friends. Such is the power of agape to transform Eve and Helen into itself.

But granted that this is so, there is the other interesting and important fact that the majority of the mystics were celibate (as was Francis who called himself God's troubadour and St. John of the Cross whose erotic poetry I have quoted) and their celibacy was an integral part of their mysticism. How explain this?

Here we must remember that while Sophia is compatible with Eve and Helen and while it transforms them, it is not identical with them. It has an existence of its own. It is a love whose source is God and whose object is God, for it is poured into our hearts by the Holy Spirit who is given to us. In its intense mystical form it sometimes appears quite suddenly in human life—as an illumination, as a direct gift from God, as a consolation without previous cause. Let me put it this way. We sometimes hear it said that: "Children cannot love unless they have received human love in an existential way—either from parents or from others." And while I believe that this is a useful psychological principle, I also ask myself: "Is it not possible for God to communicate his love directly? Must love always come through the mediation of parents and others? Cannot the unloved child have a direct experience of God's love in a mystical way? And cannot the loved child have this experience also?" And I believe that the answer is in the affirmative. I believe it frequently happens that children (and, of course, adults also) have a direct mystical experience of God's love, a consolation without previous cause. Then they know that they are loved, and they feel a tremendous thirst that cannot be assuaged or satisfied by anything human but only by the Infinite God himself.[10]

And the authentic celibate, having experienced this unrestricted love and knowing that God is its source and its object, does not reject Eve and Helen, but decides always to go beyond to the source of all love. And this decision is made in answer to a call. Obviously, the celibate mystic, like any other human person, will feel the attraction of Eve and the fascination of Helen. He or she will feel, sometimes violently, the struggle to transcend, but he or she seeks always to be guided by this experiential love that St. John of the Cross calls "the living flame of love" and which the author of *The Cloud* calls "the blind stirring of love."

This is a love that is universal, that is going out to the Infinite, that is going out to all men and women, to enemy as well as to friend; it is a love that brings much human joy. Within it there will always be an element of the transfigured Eve and the transfigured Helen; within it there will be that tenderness which filled the heart of the good Samaritan when he picked up his wounded enemy and brought him to the inn. And it is always going beyond, going beyond, to see God as he is in himself.

William James, writing at the beginning of this century, spoke of mysticism as a "feeling" rather than a rational impulse. This I believe is true. And human agape (which is also divine agape) is the most refined feeling; it is the peak point in the spiritualization of matter.

The Way of Devotion

I

I have spoken about Eve and Helen; and it remains to speak about Mary who, in Jungian symbolism, stands for devotion. It should be noted, however, that I am not here discussing the role of the Virgin Mary in the mystical life (that is another problem) but the role of that delicate and refined religious feeling that we call devotion and that Jung associates with Mary. My point is that just as there is no opposition between romantic love and agape, just as an element of a transformed romantic love is usually present in the experience of agape, so there is no opposition whatever between devotion and agape—indeed devotional love is very, very close to agape. In Sophia the transformed Virgin Mary is forever present.

While devotion plays an important role in the practice of all the great religions, it is also true that sophisticated (and sometimes less sophisticated) people tend to deemphasize devotion, considering it somehow a sign of weakness. Perhaps this is because they realize that religious feeling can be divorced from religious commitment (that is to say, can be divorced from true agape) and that it is often changeable and fickle. Or they see that religious feeling can degenerate into superstition or hysteria. Or they see that enthusiastic feelings of devotion can be a substitute for faith. And while these dangers are very real, let us not forget that the other danger that exists when devotion is abandoned in favor of pure spirit is much more insidious and devastating.

For devotion is a necessary aspect of the religious consciousness. This point is made by no less a person than Dr. D. T. Suzuki, the great authority on zen. He is speaking about Pure Land Buddhism which, he claims, is basically "unbuddhistic" and arose in Northern India centuries after the death of Shakyamuni the Buddha. Suzuki claims that this Pure Land Buddhism had to arise because primitive Buddhism was greatly lacking in affectivity—"the rise of the Pure Land idea illustrates the persistent and irrepressible assertion of certain aspects of our religious consciousness—the aspects somewhat neglected in the so-called primitive teaching of the Buddha."[11] And he goes on to say that zen, being like primitive Buddhism, needs the tender devotion of the *nembutsu* which calls upon the name of Amida. "Zen being too philosophical (though not in the ordinary sense of the term) exposed itself to an utter disregard of the emotional side of life. Zen indulges itself in excessive *satori*, so to speak, and as a result it frequently dries up its tears which must be shed over ignorance, over the miseries of life, over the world filled with iniquity. Thus zen holds out no hope of a land of bliss and purity which is so vividly felt by the followers of the *nembutsu.*"[12]

Although zen and Pure Land Buddhism are rivals, they need one another, says Suzuki—and, in particular, zen needs the Pure Land. This is clear from the history of Chinese zen; and I believe it is clear in Japan today. Many zen masters have a simple devotion to Amida; and most zen monasteries have a statue of Kannon, the illustrious and compassionate Bodhisattva who refused to enter the Pure Land until all sentient beings were saved. But Dr. Suzuki himself is a good example of a Buddhist who reconciled within himself these two apparently different streams. Shortly before his death in 1966 at the age of ninety-six, I had the privilege of hearing him lecture on the Pure Land, and I could not but be inspired by his gentle devotion and his spirit of trust in God.

Here I cannot speak in detail about Pure Land Buddhism and the great and humble Shinran who founded the Shin sect. Only let me say that Shinran (1173–1263) taught his followers one thing: They must call on the name of Amida with faith. Doing this they would be reborn in Pure Land. Faith alone is important—and one who has faith has no need of works and practices and ascetical exercises. One need not sit in the lotus; one need not embrace celibacy. Only faith in Amida will save.

And Suzuki makes the surprising claim that devotional recitation of the *nembutsu* (*Namu Amida Butsu*) leads to a realm of *satori* that is no different from that of zen. Both forms of Buddhism lead to the same self-realization. The follower of the Pure Land ends by realizing that Amida is his own mind and his own mind is Amida. In short, if Suzuki is correct, tender and devotional faith in Amida leads to the emptiness, the nothingness and the void, which are the hallmarks of the zen *satori*.

II

If devotion is central to the Buddhist religious practice, it is equally or more central in the Christian way of life. This is because Christianity is centered on commitment to Jesus, God and man. It is precisely through Jesus that one goes to the Father according to those words that Jesus cried out in the synagogue: "He who believes in me, believes not in me but in him who sent me" (John 12:44). Consequently, it is not surprising that a deeply devotional thread should run through the gospels, particularly through the fourth gospel which carefully develops the relationship between Jesus and his disciples. It is here that we see the friendships of Jesus. "Now Jesus loved Martha and her sister and Lazarus" (John 11:5). And Jesus said: "Our friend Lazarus has fallen asleep . . ." (John 11:11). And particularly important, of course, is the friendship between Jesus and the disciple whom he loved, who also lay close to his breast at the Last Supper.

It is not surprising, then, that from the earliest days any baptized Christian could call himself the disciple whom Jesus loved; and friendship with Jesus was a great ideal in the Christian life. Note, also, that the fourth gospel does not speak of the disciple who loved Jesus but of the disciple whom Jesus loved. It is of primary importance to realize that I am loved by Jesus, that I am chosen—and that my loving response is the second step. "You did not choose me, but I chose you" (John 15:16).

As I said, this loving friendship with Jesus is a central theme in primitive Christianity and it is developed in the twelfth century by Bernard of Clairvaux, who is the giant inspirer of medieval devotion and piety. To this love for Jesus, Bernard added an equally tender devotion to Mary, the mother of Jesus, a devotion that, deeply ingrained in the New Testament, grows and grows as the people of God move forward through the centuries. And these devotions are found not only in Bernard but also in à Kempis, Aquinas, Eckhart, Tauler, Suso, the author of *The Cloud*, Richard and Hugh of St. Victor and a whole galaxy of medieval mystics. We hear a good deal about Eckhart's mystical resemblance to zen, but little is said about those sermons that are filled with tender devotion to the Eucharist and to Mary, the mother of Jesus. And the author of *The Cloud*, who loves to talk about the unknowability of God, waxes eloquent about the love of Jesus for Mary Magdalen and her love for him. In this he follows a devotional tradition which goes back to Augustine.

And then, of course, there is St. Teresa of Avila. How she emphasizes that at the very peak point of the mystical life one must remain with the incarnate Jesus of Nazareth! Indeed she maintains uncompromisingly that without Jesus of Nazareth no one can enter the deepest realms of the interior castle that is the mystical life. Speaking of those who wanted to abandon Christ's humanity in order to find deeper mystical experience she writes:

> I can assure them that they will not enter these last two mansions; for, if they lose their guide, the good Jesus, they will be unable to find the way, they will do well if they are able to remain securely in the other mansions. For the Lord himself says that he is the Way; the Lord also says that He is the Light and that no one comes to the Father save by Him and that "he that seeth me seeth my Father." It may be said that these words have another meaning. I do not know of any such meaning. I myself have got on very well with the meaning my soul always feels to be the true one."[13]

Clearly Teresa is here warning people who think they will enter deeper mansions of mystical experience by side-stepping devotion to the Risen Jesus. To do so is a dead end. For Jesus is the way. Put in Jungian terms, Jesus is the central symbol of the Christian religion; Jesus is at the center of the Christian mandala. Any Christian who puts this symbol aside or chooses another will make no progress.

Such is devotion to the humanity of Jesus. Its concrete expression is reception of the Eucharist, reading of the gospels, prayer and, above all, deep love for others.

However, it is also true (and Teresa knows it well) that there may come a time when one is drawn away from thoughts and images and concepts of Jesus. There may come a time when one is called to enter the cloud of unknowing, burying beneath a "cloud of forgetting" even the most sacred thoughts and images. Now one enters into the imageless void. And where is Jesus?

And here the Christian mystical tradition asserts unanimously that one is leaving Jesus to find him in a new way. Yes, we must leave Jesus to find Jesus, writes à Kempis. And this may mean saying to the Lord: "Good-bye. I am leaving you; but I know that you are present with me in another way. And I know that I will find you luminously at the end of my journey." Again, the author of *The Cloud* describes this experience in terms of Mary Magdalen sitting at the feet of Jesus. So captivated is she by his divinity that she "forgets" his sacred humanity. Does not this image beautifully combine the warmth of devotion with the darkness of the cloud?

But let me return to the Jungian symbols. As agape grows in the silence and the darkness, Eve and Helen pass through a process of transformation. And the same can be said of the Virgin Mary. Just as the transfigured Eve and Helen stand out with dazzling beauty, so also does the transfigured Mary, who is the woman clothed with the sun.

III

Earlier in this chapter I said that most Christian mystics were celibate; and I explained their celibacy in terms of that agape which goes beyond Eve and Helen while not leaving them behind. Now let me add that celibacy in the Christian tradition has always been associated with deep and tender devotion to the Virgin Mary. One reason for this may be that Marian devotion teaches us that it is possible to love humanly and powerfully while at the same time going beyond sexual passion. Existentially it tells us something very, very important about human nature and about ourselves. And this is a lesson that is of the utmost significance not only for celibates but also for the married, for celibate love is not the monopoly of celibate people. Everyone, married or celibate, is called at times to love deeply, tenderly and radically—in a celibate way. And the devotion that the Christian has for Mary is a prototype of this love.

I have been speaking about devotion to Mary as it exists in the hearts of millions of Christians. But a further step was made by Grignon de Montfort (1673–1716) who claimed that this devotion can carry the Christian to the summit of the mystical life. I believe that this is true. But about Marian mysticism I cannot speak here.

Let me conclude by affirming once again that authentic Christian prayer is never destructive. It comes not to abolish but to fulfill. It transforms human feelings through a process that, never complete in this life, reaches fulfillment through death and resurrection.

NOTES

1. *Spiritual Exercises of St. Ignatius* Second Week, Fifth Contemplation.
2. St. Ignatius wept profusely in time of prayer and while offering the sacrifice of the mass. In his diary he writes: "Later, just before Mass, during it and after it, there was a great abundance of tears, devotion and heavy sobbing." Such entries occur again and again in his diary. See William J. Young, trans., *The Spiritual*

Journal of St. Ignatius Loyola (Woodstock, Maryland: Woodstock College Press, 1958), p. 6.
3. *The Living Flame of Love*, st. 3.³
4. *The Dark Night*, st. 5.
5. C. G. Jung, *Collected Works*, Vol.16, *The Practice of Psychotherapy* (London: Routledge and Kegan Paul, 1966), p. 174.
6. C. S. Lewis, *The Allegory of Love* (Oxford, Eng.: Oxford University Press, 1936), p. 4.
7. Ibid., p. 2.
8. See especially Denis de Rougement, *Love in the Western World* (New York: Doubleday, 1957). This is a translation of *L'Amour et L'Occident*, published in France in 1939. Martin D'Arcy summarizes the contents: "In this book de Rougemont dares what Lewis refrained from doing: he tries to explain why the love of the romantics is so different from that of Christian love;—and here the surprise comes—the reason given is that romantic love springs from an unholy and forbidden source, the strange, wild Eros, the necromancing and unbaptized witch, who is an implacable foe of Christianity and ever seeks to cast her spells over the true lover. There are two loves, so de Rougemont holds, which fight for man's soul, Eros and Agape, and each has its own definite characteristics which enable us to recognize it." See *The Mind and Heart of Love* by M. C. D'Arcy (New York: Holt, 1947), p. 28.
9. *The Dark Night*, st. 6.
10. The medievals said that God sometimes communicates himself "without mean" (*sine medio*) and the author of *The Cloud* speaks of a love that is inspired not by any intermediary but by "the loveliness of God in himself." This is the "consolation without previous cause" of St. Ignatius. I have written about this communication "without mean" in *The Mysticism of 'The Cloud of Unknowing*,' p. 108.
11. D. T. Suzuki, *Indian Mahayana Buddhism*, ed. Edward Conze (New York: Harper & Row, 1968), p. 131.
12. *Ibid.*, p. 151. The word *nembutsu* means literally "to think of the Buddha." It consists in reciting the formula: *Namu Amida Butsu:* "Adoration to the Buddha."
13. St. Teresa of Avila, *The Interior Castle*, trans. Allison Peers (New York: Doubleday Image Books, 1961), "Sixth Mansion," chap. 7. In the same chapter Teresa urges people not to make efforts to remain constantly in the prayer of quiet: "The good Jesus is too good company for us to forsake Him and His most sacred Mother." I have discussed St. Teresa's approach to the humanity of Christ in *Silent Music*, Part II, chap. 7.

7

Healing and Redemption

A LL THE GREAT religions agree that human nature is basically wounded and stands drastically in need of healing. Buddhism speaks of the wound that is illusion and of the healing that
comes through enlightenment. And popular Buddhism sets before
our eyes statues of the healing Buddha (*Yakushi Nyorai*), the Lord of
the world of pure emerald in the East, who has vowed to cure diseases
and who is represented holding medicine in his compassionately
outstretched hand. And all this is paralleled in Christianity. Here we
learn of original sin and of justification through faith in the blood of
Jesus Christ. Moreover, recent Christianity has witnessed the rise of
a great and beautiful devotion to Jesus the healer. Valid and attractive
as this devotion is, however, we must always recall that the healings
of Jesus are not only compassionate acts of mercy towards the sick
and afflicted; they are also, and more profoundly, signs of the final
healing he came to bring. This final healing is salvation, redemption,
the ultimate healing.

The Christian mystics do not speak much about healing; but they
speak eloquently about purification, which is more or less the same
thing. For this purification is not only a liberation from "faults," not
only an ethical reformation but also a healing of neuroses and fears

and anxieties and hang-ups of all kinds. It is a healing of the senses and a transformation of the body. Nor is it simply a patching-up job, a work of repair through which the malignant tumor is removed. No, no, it is a transfiguration and a building up of something wonderfully new.

The contemplative process through which this healing takes place is rather similar in the mysticisms of the great religions. So let me refer first to a way of meditation employed in primitive Buddhism, and afterwards I shall treat more fully of the corresponding Christian process.

The Way of Healing of the Memory

I

In primitive Buddhism we hear of a technique of traveling back in time or in memory, retracing the days and months and years until one can relive one's past lives, until one arrives at the origin of all things—"thus one reaches the paradoxical moment beyond which time did not exist because nothing was yet manifested."[1] As can readily be seen, there is here something corresponding to the discovery of one's original face in zen.

And this form of meditation is not just an interesting enterprise. It aims at healing. "To relive one's past lives," writes Mircea Eliade, "is equivalent to understanding them, and, in a certain measure, to 'burning' one's 'sins'—the sum, that is, of the acts performed under the domination of ignorance and transmitted from life to life by the law of *karma*."[2] And through this healing one enters *nirvana* and is saved.

A somewhat similar method, Eliade tells us, is found in tantrism. Here the process leads to "the coincidence of time and eternity, of *bhava* and *nirvana*; on the purely human plane, of male and female—in a word, the reconquest of the completeness that precedes all creation."[3] And my reader will immediately see how this resembles the union of the *yin* and the *yang* and the return to the Tao. Here is the ultimate Buddhist healing. Here is Buddhist salvation.

And, needless to say, this resonates with much modern therapy, which centers around the human memory and seeks to heal not only the wounds of childhood and the trauma of birth but also the prenatal life and the wounds inflicted upon the fetus in the womb.

II

But now let me look at the healing of the memory through Christian contemplation.

As the contemplative life develops, it simplifies. Words become fewer; silence predominates; inner words rise up from the deeper areas of the psyche and from the center of the soul. And at this time other things also surface from the unconscious, things that need to be healed—suppressed fears, anguish, all kinds of hurts. Now one continues to sit in the presence of God in a situation that is paradoxically filled with joy and filled with anguish. Here there is a strange mixture of peace and pain.

And this is the beginning of the dark night. Now I must not push these hurts into the unconscious; I must not bury them; I must not flee from the ghosts and the dragons and the wild beasts that leer and smirk and grimace. It does not help to run away either to watch television or to play golf or to throw myself into frenetic work. However laudable these activities in themselves, now is not the time for them. Now is the time to sit quietly with God even when the whole inner life becomes desperately painful, even when all hell seems to break loose inside me. I must let it all surface; I must face the devil. But (and this is important) while I *watch* all this material as it comes up, I must not *analyze* it or *get involved* with it. I must not be seduced by the wild figures from the unconscious; I must not let them engage me in treacherous dialogue. No, no. I must remain with God in the cloud of unknowing, simply watching them and watching myself with compassion.

Painful, you will say. Yes, very painful. For in this process I am vividly reliving the past with all its sorrow and anguish. I am, of course, going through this agony in the presence of a God who loves me and has always protected me. And here is my strength. But together with the support that comes from God's love and grace I ordinarily need human support from a loving friend or counselor or director—from one who will listen, accept, reflect back to me what is happening. Fortunate am I when I find such a compassionate mirror that will accept me into its depths and reflect back with love what is happening in my life.

But the suffering and pain need not disturb me. It has to be so. There seems to be a direct relationship between healing and suffering. In order to be healed one must suffer; one must *undergo*. That is why, after speaking about the healings of Jesus, Matthew refers to Isaiah: "This was to fulfil what was spoken by the prophet Isaiah, 'He took our infirmities and bore our diseases'" (Matt. 8:17). Yes, Jesus had to suffer, not for his own wounds but for ours.

And through this painful process the memory is being healed. The hurts and pains that have been lurking in the psyche from early childhood, from the moment of birth, from the time in the womb, from the moment of conception—all of these are floating to the surface and are being healed by the love of the indwelling Spirit in whose presence one quietly sits. Furthermore, while I myself cannot accept a literal interpretation of the Buddhist doctrine of past lives and of liberation from bad *karma*, I think I understand what Buddhists are driving at; and I see there a valuable insight. For I believe that there takes place a healing of something more than my little ego with its memory of a mere forty, fifty or sixty years. There is more to it than this. There is a healing of the archetypes, of the collective unconscious, of the wounds I have inherited from my ancestors. There is a healing of the cosmic dimension of the psyche; there is a healing of the basic human condition which we call original sin.

And this, again, can be a harrowing experience. For no wild beast on the face of the earth can compare with the archetypal evil that can emerge from the depths of the collective unconscious. One's great consolation lies in the fact that deeper than this stark evil is the image of God and the beauty of one's true self, which will eventually shine forth when the other evil has evaporated. But, I need hardly say, original sin is never totally healed in this life; we never cease to be the dried shit-stick of Unmon.

III

I like to look at this healing in terms of those transcendental precepts to which I have appealed several times. For the first step is *be atten-*

tive. In contemplation I am listening to myself, to my deepest and most beautiful center where God is enshrined; but I am also listening to the garbage that is arising first from my personal unconscious and then from my collective unconscious. I am facing up to the truth about myself, and the truth is making me free. In the second step I am coming to *understand* myself. And psychologists agree that understanding is immensely healing. When I come to understand what happened in my life, when I come to understand my childhood relationship with my parents or with my environment—then a measure of healing is already accomplished. In the third step I objectivize the problem, speak about it to another, and really *know* it. Now I see meaning, and logotherapy rightly claims that one who sees meaning is immensely liberated.

Here, however, let me pause to say that for effective healing all the problems need not be explicitly known as they are known in therapy. As we sit in silent contemplation, healing (sometimes painful healing) is taking place without our knowing explicitly what we are being healed from. We recognize that some repressed wound is there; we feel the turbulence and the anguish; but we cannot label it. We do not know exactly what it is; and we don't always need to know, for it is healed without our explicit knowledge. Such was the healing that took place in the lives of Christian contemplatives before the great psychoanalytic discoveries. The old contemplatives tell us how they suddenly (or gradually) felt a new sense of liberation, of joy, of inner strength. They did not know explicitly that this was a healing of childhood memories or infantile fixations, but in many cases it was precisely that. But let me return to the healing process.

Understanding and knowledge, however valuable, are not enough to accomplish healing. The great healer is *love.* And in our case this is the contemplative love poured into our hearts by the Holy Spirit who is given to us. This is the agape that is the glory of the Christian life; it is the gift of God, and as it goes out towards all men and women, so it goes out towards one's self. As we love all men and women, so we love ourselves. As we forgive others, so we forgive ourselves. And here, I believe, we are at the hub of the whole problem. Modern psychology reminds us that too, too many people hate themselves, punish themselves, flagellate themselves, refuse to forgive themselves. They are angry with themselves or their parents or their friends, and they feel guilty because of their anger. If only they could expose the whole thing to the love of God so as to receive forgiveness and to forgive themselves and others, what a release from guilt would be effected and what joy would flood their being

For liberation from guilt and forgiveness of self bring a wonderful self-acceptance and great joy. Even if I see that I am covered with wounds I can laugh and rejoice. With Paul I can glory in this weakness through which the strength of Christ shines most vibrantly. And here is the great healing.

Let me pause here to make a personal comment. I used to think that the great saints of East and West were liberated from all fear and clinging and that they had, so to speak, arrived. Now I see that such a way of thinking is illusory. The greatest saint or sage is weak; the greatest saint or sage has his problems and his falls. His greatness is not in his supreme liberation but in his recognition of his own nothingness. And he must never forget that the healing is effected not through his own efforts but through the grace of Another.

IV

But let me look more closely at the wounds. They can be broadly divided into two categories. In the first category are the wounds that arise from our relationships with other people, going back to childhood and to the womb. Among these the most damaging are sustained anger or lack of forgiveness. When I nourish anger (even unconsciously) I damage myself more than the person I hate. And so the healing consists in letting the resentment surface and float away, to be replaced by love and compassion and forgiveness; or the healing may consist in letting this anger be transformed into a passionate thirst for justice. But together with this anger will be other frustrations—tears not shed, fear not expressed, shocks rammed into the unconscious, traumas half-forgotten, sexual repressions. And these may have been greatly intensified by the exterior situation—by a childhood lived in a police state, or by a situation of violence, or by being politically uprooted or rejected. The thought of the psychological wounds inflicted on children in the modern world boggles the mind and makes one ask: "How can it all be healed?" And yet there is the strange paradox that people raised in these dreadful circumstances are sometimes healthier than the affluent. A friend of mine who worked with refugees in Cambodia remarked: "I saw that we, the helpers, were just as wounded as the refugees—but in a different way."

However, when all these wounds have been faced and healed or accepted, we are still face to face with the deepest wound of all; namely, our relationship with the Absolute. This is the most basic problem in human life and it underlies all other problems. Buddhism speaks of it in its own terms. It speaks of the great illusion that is our "separated self "; it speaks of the destructive isolation that comes from building up the ego. And parallel to this is the Christian problem of separation from God and the great need of reconciliation and redemption. In the concrete, this problem may again take the form of a deep self-hatred by which I cut myself off from others, from the totality of things and from God. I have already said that modern psychology has brought to light the sad fact that many, many people hate themselves and are convinced that they are not lovable. This makes them ward off not only the love of other people but also the love of God. Like Adam and Eve they shamefully run away. What a wound this is! And I believe it can only be healed when, through the grace of Christ, we learn to open our hearts to receive love, both human and divine. If we do this, a time will come when, either in a flash or by degrees, we will come to realize existentially that we are forgiven, loved by God, chosen from eternity, redeemed by Jesus Christ, called by name. Then we will be liberated with great joy. And only then, when our relationship with God is put right, will our human relationships be healed.

V

Corresponding to the healing of our relationships with other people and our relationship with God are the two nights of the Christian mystics. The first night centers around affectivity, sexuality, relationships with others. But the second night centers around the so-called theological virtues of faith, hope and charity, by which we relate directly to God. It deprives us of all securities so that we can say that we believe in God for God, hope in God for God, love God for God.

St. John of the Cross treats these two nights separately and systematically. But he writes like a man in a hurry, for he does not want to waste time on the first night. There are enough books about it. Much more significant is the second night, the night of faith, in which the soul is transformed in God. Yes, the healing of this second night is nothing less than the divinization of the human person. Redemption is precisely that. God became man to redeem us: God became man in order that man might become God. That is why Paul can say that the free gift is much greater than the trespass, as if to say that the healing is much more wonderful than the elimination of the wound.

And one more point. The Spanish mystics speak constantly about a very special wound, a wound of love. There comes a time in their experience when they are wounded by God. They get a glimpse of the divine beauty, and then they are consumed with a longing and a thirst for God that can only be assuaged by vision. It is then that they cry that they are sick with love; it is then that they quote the Song of Songs:

> Upon my bed by night
> I sought him whom my soul loves
> I sought him, but found him not;
> I called him, but he gave no answer. [Cant. 3:1]

The poetry of St. John of the Cross centers around this wound that can only be healed by the vision of the beloved. Anything less than God is just a messenger, and he cries out with holy frustration: "Do not send me any more messengers; they cannot tell me what I must bear."[4]

And so we find a longing for death and resurrection. For the mystic realizes that this is the supreme healing. And it will come. It will come when "God . . . will wipe away every tear from their eyes, and death shall be no more, neither shall there be any mourning nor crying nor pain any more, for the former things have passed away" (Rev. 21:4).

From the Womb to the Tomb

I

From what has been said it will be clear that in both Buddhism and

139

Christianity healing of the memory is of cardinal importance in the path of salvation. And what a mystery is the human memory! How full of beauty and how full of garbage! This wonderful human faculty has been damaged from the dawn of consciousness—damaged from the time of conception and from the moment we were born of sinful parents into a sinful world. Can we not all cry out with the psalmist: "Behold I was brought forth in iniquity, and in sin did my mother conceive me" (Ps. 51:5)? And have we not grown up in a world where hurt and rejection and suffering are part of the process of living? And does not Paul speak of a world that has been subjected to the powers of darkness?

Yet this same world has been created by a loving Father and redeemed by a loving Savior. As hurt is part of the process of living, so also is healing. We all experience at times the spontaneous healing power inherent in the human mind and body. We know that hurts and injuries, both spiritual and physical, heal themselves; we know that we grow out of our problems—even though the basic wound called original sin remains until the end.

And then there is the healing power of meditation about which I have been speaking. I can sit or stand before God, exposing the wounded memory to the healing love that comes through the merits of Jesus Christ. In this way I relive the past. I experience vividly and existentially that God was present in all that happened. I know with certainty that all will be well. Something like this is done daily by those people who practice the so-called examination of conscience. For a long time this "examen" was regarded as a fault-finding mission, a guilty search for one's sins, but more recently we come to see it as an "examination of consciousness" in which one comes to look for the action of God in one's consciousness—and becomes aware of the activity that is not from God. This is indeed a healing process.

At other times one can see that God was present in everything that happened since one's life in the womb. Here let me say that one can have access to the life of the womb in two ways. The first way is by recalling those symbolical dreams that carry the data of the prenatal life. The other way is through mystical experience that touches those levels of consciousness that are ordinarily deeply buried. It is indeed interesting to see how many religious and mystical writers are sensitively aware of the life in the womb. Think of the Bardo Thödol (*The*

Tibetan Book of the Dead) with its vivid descriptions that make one
think that the author was recalling his own prenatal life. And then
the psalmist:

> For thou didst form my inward parts,
> Thou didst knit me together in my mother's womb. [Ps. 149:13]

Is the psalmist here speaking of something he has learned about from
others? Or of something he remembers? And in yet another psalm
he looks back in memory and cries:

> Yet thou art he who took me from the womb;
> Thou didst keep me safe upon my mother's breasts.
> Upon thee was I cast from birth,
> And since my mother bore me thou hast been my God. [Ps. 22:9]

Highly enlightened people, whose memory has been healed and
purified from blockages and fears and hurts, can have a panoramic
vision that goes back to the very act of love by which their parents
gave them life. Such a vision is not unlike that which frequently
occurs at the moment of death. If it is accompanied by faith, in such
wise that one sees the action of God in all that happened, it can be
immensely healing.

II

But in order to understand the human memory it is helpful to reflect
on the so-called life cycle which has fascinated many eminent psychologists in our day. This is the journey from the womb to the tomb
with its crises or passages, with its deaths and resurrections. A
consideration of these in the light of the gospel helps us to see how
the human memory is hurt and healed, hurt and healed, hurt and
healed, until it is finally liberated through death. Following Jung,
then, let me speak of four crises: birth, adolescence, mid-life and
death.

The first crisis, beginning when one emerges from the womb,
extends over the first six or seven years of life. It has been preceded
by a period of total dependence on the mother, in whose loving womb
the child has been formed. This child may already have had its shocks

and fears; and now comes the trauma of birth. I need not speak about the necessity of breaking the umbilical cord, about saying good-bye to one's mother, about radically starting on the journey towards maturity. Enough has been written about that.

The second crisis comes with adolescence. Now is the time to become independent, to stand on one's own feet, to relate to parents no longer as a child but as an adult. Often this is a time of an abrupt break with parental authority, a time of struggle and emotional storm. And here it is interesting to observe how the great religions, notably Judaism, Christianity and Confucianism, help believers to cop: with this crisis in that they stress the value of mature love and reverence for parents and ancestors. What psychology since Freud has most of all stressed is that such filial piety does not come easily. It is the fruit of struggle and suffering, and sometimes it comes late in life when parents are long since dead. But psychology has also told us that filial piety is the key to emotional maturity and even to sexual identity.

But if damaged, how is this filial relationship healed?

We have heard a lot about accepting one's parents and accepting oneself, about forgiving and being forgiven, about reliving a wounded relationship in fantasy. And all this is very good and very healing. But it is not enough. For our relationship with father and mother is based on an archetypal life that has also been injured by original sin and the wounds of life. Yes, it is the *father image* and the *mother image* that must be healed. And I myself believe that in the Christian life this healing is effected by a filial devotion to God as Father and a tender love for Mary as Mother. When, through the experience of love for God and for the mother of God, one's archetypes are healed, it becomes possible to relate in an authentic and beautiful way to one's earthly father and mother. Now one recognizes their human faults and imperfections; one understands the problems with which they struggled, and one truly honors them as persons and as supreme benefactors.

And what I say of the father and mother archetypes holds true for other human archetypes. Washed by the waters of baptism, nourished by the body and blood of Christ, forgiven through the sacrament of reconciliation, committed Christians are healed in this deep archetypal area upon which the whole human fabric is built.

What I say here, of course, is based on Jungian psychology, and let me make the observation that Jung was enamored of the Catholic devotion to Mary. He was aware that the mother archetype was disastrously neglected in some religions; and he clapped his hands with joy when the Catholic church defined the doctrine of Mary's assumption into heaven. Clearly he saw the therapeutic dimension of devotion to Mary, and he felt happy about her exaltation.

III

But let me pass on to the third crisis, which is that of middle age. This, I believe, is primarily a religious crisis. Jung indicates this in a remarkable passage in which he speaks of patients over the age of thirty-five:

> I should like to call attention to the following facts. During the past thirty years, people from all the civilized countries of the earth have consulted me. Many hundreds of patients have passed through my hands, the greater number being Protestants, a lesser number Jews, and not more than five or six believing Catholics. Among all my patients in the second half of life—that is to say, over thirty-five—there has not been one whose problem in the last resort was not that of finding a religious outlook on life. It is safe to say that every one of them fell ill because he had lost what the living religions of every age have given their followers, and none of them has been really healed who did not regain his religious outlook.[5]

The mid-life crisis is one of meaning. One is searching, searching, searching for meaning. Jung believed that the great religions give the meaning for which the middle-aged person craves. Furthermore, if the earlier crises center around interpersonal relations (and, in particular, around the relationship with one's parents) the mid-life crisis centers around one's relationship with God. It is at this time that one discovers the insufficiency of even the most beautiful human relationship. One realizes with Augustine that our hearts were made for God and are restless until they rest in him; this is the time when one may exclaim that only God can help me now, because vain is the help of man or woman. Again, if the earlier crises concern the first night, the night of the senses, the mid-life crisis concerns the second night, the night of faith. It is here again that one is most likely to resonate with the *lama sabach-thani* (Matt. 27:46).

The final crisis is death. About this we know little, but growing evidence points to death as a time of potential enlightenment, a time of growth, a time of healing—one may have a panoramic view of the past and a joyful surrender to the future. In a sense all other crises look forward to this one, for they are all death-and-resurrection experiences. But can we prepare for death in such wise that it will be truly and profoundly healing?

The *Bardo Thödol* provides a ritual in which the lama, standing beside the dying person, utters words of warning and words of consolation into his or her ear. It reminds one of the medieval *Ars Moriendi* or *Art of Dying* and of the last rites ministered through the Catholic liturgy today. The *Bardo Thödol* is clear in its assertion that the dying person is confronted with two possibilities: either to reenter a maternal womb for further purification in the drama of a new life, or to enter *nirvana*, thus winning liberation from the cycle of birth and death. But the final liberation comes not from personal effort but from the grace of Amida.

Now again, while I myself do not accept the doctrine of reincarnation, I nevertheless see here some important and valuable insights. The first is that we cannot be finally liberated by our own efforts but only by grace. The old Christian authors stressed this when they spoke of "the grace of final perseverance," meaning that no one merits this final liberation or attains to it by his or her own efforts. It is a gratuitous gift of a merciful God.

Second, in the doctrine of reincarnation in order to be purified and liberated from bad *karma* so as finally to enter *nirvana*, I see a parallel to the Catholic doctrine of purgatory. This latter holds that many, or most, people must undergo a period of purification prior to their definitive entry into eternal life.

Third, I see something important in the Buddhist belief that one does not find salvation within the cycle of life-death-life-death that is called *samsara*, for salvation is outside of that. Put in concrete terms, we may travel back in time with a psychiatrist; we may relive all the wounds back to the time of conception; but it is only when we are brought beyond our life in the womb to our existence in the mind of God that we can be healed. Salvation does not come from within the human memory but from outside.

In short, we are only healed when, like Jeremiah, we hear addressed to ourselves those words of love and of choice: "Before I formed you in the womb I knew you . . ." (Jer. 1:5). Yes, before I was conceived God knew and loved me. "From the body of my mother he named my name . . ." (Isa. 49:1). This is the voice that enters the Christian's life, not dramatically but in a quiet and simple way. It is the voice to which the Christian answers with words: "Our Father . . . "

And this voice can make itself heard at various times in human life. Jeremiah heard it as a teenager and protested that he was too young to follow its dictates. But he hears the same voice many times during his life. And we, too, may hear it many times. But however frequently or infrequently we hear that voice in our daily life, we all hope to hear it at the moment of death. For that is the supreme time of the knocking at the door. That is the time when we wish to cry out: "Come, Lord Jesus . . . " (Rev. 22:20).

But my point here is that no one can force that voice. No one can claim the right to hear it. The initiative comes from beyond. Salvation is a gift.

Jung: West and East

I

Jung was acutely aware of the collective sickness and the collective evil of the world in which he lived. He saw the rise and fall of Nazism; he saw the concentration camps and the liquidation of the Jews; he saw the destruction of Dresden; he saw the holocausts of Hiroshima and Nagasaki. And for him all this evil was the reflection of a human unconscious that was full of gruesome and violent barbarities—barbarities that spilled over the earth in the terrible conflagration of the 1940s. Put in Christian terms, the violence of the world was a reflection of the original and personal sin that darkens the human mind and heart.

Jung was particularly aware of the sickness of the Western mind, and in an interesting passage he attributes this illness partly to the violent repression of instincts that accompanied the rise of Christianity:

> We must never forget our historical premises. Only a little more than a thousand years ago we stumbled from the crudest beginnings of polytheism into the midst of a highly developed Oriental religion which lifted the imaginative minds of half-savages to a height that did not correspond to their degree of spiritual development. In order to maintain this height in some fashion or other, *the instinctual sphere had to be repressed to a great extent. . . . The repressed elements naturally do not develop, but vegetate further in their original barbarism in the unconscious.* [6]

It was this repressed barbarism that broke out in the years between 1939 and 1945, creating the awful material and spiritual havoc we have seen.

Closely allied to this way of thinking is Jung's theory of the split in the Western mind. The conscious mind of Western man, he held, was highly developed through science, philosophy, theology. Great things had been done by the scientific mind (and Jung was the last to deny it), but the unconscious lagged behind. It did not develop in a corresponding way. While the conscious mind soared to the heavens with beautiful ideas and ideals, the unconscious was a cesspool of barbarism. Put in other terms the Western *yang* was full of beauty, while the *yin* was full of ugliness. The mind was drastically split.

II

And, of course, the question arises: How can this barbaric unconscious be healed?

And to this Jung answers that Western man's unconscious "is still loaded with those contents *which must first become conscious before he can be liberated from them.*" [7] And this is one central thrust of Jungian psychology: "Make the unconscious conscious. Or, more correctly, allow the unconscious to become conscious! Bring things out into the open! Let the ugly contents of the unconscious surface!" This can be done by psychoanalysis, by reflecting on one's dreams, but it is done principally through the art of allowing growth to take place within the psyche. In this context Jung quotes a letter from one of his patients who describes how "by keeping quiet, repressing nothing, remaining attentive, and by accepting reality—taking things as they are, and not as I wanted them to be," she had come to a new degree of consciousness. "So now I intend to play the game of life, being receptive to whatever comes to me, good and bad, sun and shadow that are forever alternating, and, in this way also accepting my own nature with its positive and negative sides."[8]

My reader will observe that this is very similar to the non-action or *wu-wei* of Taoism, to the way of zen, to the process of Christian contemplation. In all these forms of meditation one sits quietly and allows things to happen or (in Christian terms) one allows God to act and does not fight against the potter (Isa. 64:8). So in fact Jung is advocating nothing less than a movement towards contemplation as the supreme therapy for the cleansing of the unconscious. "This attitude is religious in the truest sense, and therefore therapeutic, for all religions are therapies for the sorrows and disorders of the soul."[9]

III

I have said that the way Jung recommends is found in Christian contemplation. And that is so. But at the time Jung was writing, Christian contemplation was little known outside of convents and monasteries. The result was that many spiritual searchers in the West, seeing mysticism as the exclusive monopoly of oriental religions, turned to zen and yoga and Tibetan mysticism. Here, they thought, was a way that would heal their wounds and lead to the spiritual experience they craved.

Jung saw this turning towards the East, and it made him uneasy. His own attitude towards Eastern religions was ambivalent. On the one hand he was enthusiastically eloquent about the achievements of the oriental mind; on the other hand, he was very, very wary about the use of zen and yoga by Westerners. For one thing he did not like to see Westerners abandon their own tradition. There is a note of poetic anger in his cry: "Of what use is the wisdom of the Upanishads or the insights of Chinese yoga, if we desert the foundations of our own culture as though they were errors outlived and, like homeless pirates, settle with thievish intent on foreign shores?"[10]

He felt, moreover, that Western man was psychologically unsuited to oriental meditation and would misuse it. "He will infallibly make a wrong use of yoga, because his psychic disposition is quite different from that of the Oriental. I say to whomsoever I can: 'Study yoga— you will learn an infinite amount from it—but do not try to apply it, for we Europeans are not so constituted that we apply these methods correctly, just like that.' "[11]

One who reads Jung carefully, however, sees that his objections to oriental meditation for Westerners were not just based on cultural differences between East and West. There was something more important. He saw that one cannot take oriental practice without oriental faith. "Yoga practice is unthinkable, and would also be ineffectual," he wrote, "without the ideas on which it is based."[12] And with a touch of humor he again writes:

> And I wish particularly to warn against the oft-attempted imitation of Indian practices and sentiments. As a rule nothing comes of it except an artificial stultification of our Western intelligence. Of course, if anyone should succeed in giving up Europe from every point of view, and could actually *be* nothing but a yogi and sit in the lotus position with all the practical and ethical consequences that this entails, evaporating on a gazelle-skin under a dusty banyan tree and ending his days in nameless non-being, then I should have to admit that such a person understood yoga in the Indian manner. But anyone who cannot do this should not behave as if he did.[13]

And the problem is precisely here. Jung saw well that the Eastern religions can use the unconscious mind to develop extraordinary powers of all kinds. He was familiar with *kundalini;* he knew about the psychic powers known as *siddhis;* he knew the great human potential unleashed through the practice of yoga; and he saw that Western man would tragically misuse this power. Whereas the Hindu who practices traditional yoga is protected by a beautiful underlying faith that inculcates nonviolence, no-stealing, love for truth, chastity, compassion and a host of virtues, the Westerner would jettison all this virtuous talk and would use the power to blow up the world, to pollute the atmosphere and to destroy himself. "As a European," he wrote, "I cannot wish the European man more 'control' and more power over the nature within us and around us."[14]

IV

How prophetic was Jung in all this! Westerners are doing precisely what he said they would do. And, alas, Orientals are following suit. They are separating the power from the underlying faith. Let us hope they will never use these psychic powers to create the ultimate weapon.

Jung saw clearly that in order to meditate wisely and effectively one must have a faith, a religion, a myth. And so he advised Westerners to dialogue with oriental religions while finding their roots in their own tradition. "The wisdom and mysticism of the East," he wrote, "serve to remind us that we in our culture possess something similar which we have already forgotten."[15] And elsewhere he made a famous statement: "In course of the centuries the West will produce its own yoga and it will be on the basis laid down by Christianity."[16]

And is the West producing its own yoga?

I would prefer to qualify the statement of Jung; for the world has moved since he penned his words of wisdom. Christianity is no longer a Western thing looking towards the East. Already there are millions of Indian Christians in the subcontinent and some of these are creating their own yoga—which is not Western but Christian. And in the same way Japanese Christians are creating, and will create, their own zen. As for Western Christianity, while remaining true to its own past it w000190 A their own yoga—which is not Western but Christian. And in the same way Japanese Christians are creating, and will create, their own zen. As for Western Christianity, while remaining true to its own past it will profit from the fruits of oriental Christianity to create a neo-mysticism. This we already see and I believe it is one of the most hopeful aspects of modern Christianity.

Redemption

But let me return to the healing power of contemplation. If Jung is correct and if we take him seriously, we must allow the barbarism that is in the unconscious to come to the surface. This means that we must live it—without repression. It means that we must accept all the violence and ugliness and fear and cruelty and we must identify with it all. What a prospect! What suffering is entailed in this! If it is already terrible to face and accept the hurt and injury and evil that is in our personal unconscious, how much more terrible to face the archetypal evil of the collective unconscious! How terrible to face the cries of the afflicted and the evil of the oppressor from the dawn of human consciousness! How terrible to identify with all this!

Yet I believe, with Jung, that it must be done. And I believe that one man has done it. I believe that one man took upon himself the suffering and sin of the world. This was one who sweated blood in the garden of Gethsemane. "For our sake he made him to be sin who knew no sin, so that in him we might become the righteousness of God" (2 Cor. 5:21). Jesus is the lamb of God who takes away the sin of the world. But in doing so he plumbed the depth of human weakness, of human suffering, of human evil. "Eli, Eli, lama sabach-thani" (Matt. 27:46). "But he was wounded for our transgressions, he was bruised for our iniquities; upon him was the chastisement that made us whole, and with his stripes we are healed" (Isa. 53:5).

Jesus has faced all this suffering and evil; he has identified with it; and through him we are saved. And the Christian mystics are those who identify with Jesus in a very radical way, for they cry out with Paul: "I complete what is lacking in Christ's afflictions for the sake of his body, that is, the church . . ." (Col. 1:24). And so they can say with Paul that they rejoice in their sufferings and glory in the cross of our Lord Jesus; and their great ideal is to share his sufferings, becoming like him in his death, that if possible they may attain the resurrection of the dead (Phil. 3:10).

Concretely, they identify with Jesus and allow the suffering of the personal unconscious to surface—and that is the first night. They also allow the suffering of the collective unconscious to surface—and that is the second night. In this second night they identify with the cries of the poor and the agony of the human race. No longer preoccupied with their own little egos and their own little sufferings they have become universal persons and take on themselves the agony of the world.

And in this way they become other Christs. They become saviors as Jesus was the Savior. As Jesus was divine by nature, they are divine by grace. As Jesus conquered death and suffering, so they also conquer death and suffering. As Jesus died and rose, so they die and rise. And thanks to their union with Jesus we are healed and saved.

NOTES

1. Mircea Eliade, *Yoga: Immortality and Freedom* (Princeton, N.J.: Princeton University Press, 1969), p. 184.
2. Ibid., p. 185.
3. Ibid., p. 271.
4. *The Spiritual Canticle*, st. 6.
5. C. G. Jung, *Collected Works*, Vol.11 (London: Routledge and Kegan Paul, 1966), p. 334.
6. *Collected Works*, Vol.13, p. 47.
7. Ibid.
8. Ibid.
9. Ibid., p. 48.
10. *Collected Works*, Vol.15, p. 58.
11. *Collected Works*, Vol.11, p. 534.
12. Ibid., p. 533.
13. Ibid., p. 568.
14. Ibid., p. 534.
15. Ibid., p. 585.
16. Ibid., p. 537.

8

Love: Human and Divine

M ODERN MEN AND women are greatly interested in interpersonal relations, in friendship and in love. We are convinced
that there is no greater joy than that of understanding and being
understood; we know that there is no greater ecstasy than that of
loving and being loved. But we also see that deep involvement with
other people is a terrible risk that necessarily brings anguish and
suffering in its train. Yes, if we would be intimate we must pay the
price. And a high price it is. For modern literature and life keep
reminding us of the failures—of superficial relationships, casual en-
counters, broken marriages, infidelity in friendship, betrayal in love.
It is a sad, sad song. And it gives rise to gnawing doubts and painful
questions: Are deep human relationships possible? Can one make a
permanent commitment to another person or to a community? Have
perpetual vows any meaning? Does human fidelity really exist? Is the
ecstasy of a permanent love affair anything more than the euphoric
dream of romantic fools?

The Sacramental Dimension

I

And once again people look to the great religions for an answer. For it is clear that there is a religious or sacramental dimension to human relationships. This is particularly true of marriage, which in all religions is surrounded with sacred ceremony. But it is also true of spiritual guidance which, ideally speaking, is a religious encounter between two people who meet at the core of their being in an atmosphere of love and trust. Think of the oriental master. A highly enlightened person, he is leading his disciple to an enlightenment like his own. He is the transparent mirror in which the disciple sees his true self; and often the awakening or realization of the true self will take place during their brief encounter. The master has a great love which is so free from all clinging and attachment that it sometimes inspires him to send his disciple far away. As for the disciple, he is ready to die for his master. And between them is a silken bond that time and distance cannot sever: it is never broken. Beginning in a vertical way, this relationship culminates in equality; master and disciple face one another like two mirrors reflecting their mutual emptiness.

I heard of a Hindu guru who went to the West to study the spiritual guidance of Jesus in the fourth gospel. This is indeed a fascinating topic. What a profound religious experience it was to meet Jesus and to ask: "Rabbi (which means Teacher), where are you staying?" (John 1:38). And this master-disciple relationship develops into an extraordinary friendship: "No longer do I call you servants, for the servant does not know what his master is doing; but I have called you friends . . ." (John 15:15). So open is Jesus with his disciples that he can say that all he has heard from his Father he has made known to them. So free from clinging is Jesus that he can say that the disciples belong to the Father: "Thine they were, and thou gavest them to me" (John 17:6). As for the disciples, they protest that they are willing to die for Jesus, even though in the crisis their human weakness wins. And in the end there is a mutual indwelling whereby the disciples dwell in Jesus and Jesus in them like the branches in the vine and the vine in the branches. No longer are there barriers between Jesus and his own. He is the mirror in which they see themselves and in which they see the Father.

At other times the direction of Jesus is more transient in nature, as with the woman taken in adultery. And then there is that beautiful scene in which the woman kneeling at the feet of Jesus washes his feet with her tears and dries them with her hair. "Therefore I tell you, her sins, which are many, are forgiven, for she loved much . . ." (Luke 7:47). Love, forgiveness, healing, in a personal encounter with the Lord!

And similar experiences have occurred again and again in the Catholic confessional where people have been healed and reconciled and forgiven, often with tears, in the sacred encounter with another person. Or again, in spiritual direction it has frequently happened that two people have suddenly awakened to the fact that there exists between them an immense love filled with the presence of God, a love that is far beyond anything sensible or intellectual because it issues from those hidden depths that we call the center of the soul. This love envelops the mind and heart and body with a totality that makes people say: "How is it possible to love so much?" Or they can exclaim with Jeanne Frances de Chantal: "Our love has no name in any language," as if to say that this love is so different from what is usually called love that it needs another name.

II

For the fact is that there exists in this world a kind of love that is both human and divine. This is the love about which we learn in Deuteronomy: " . . .And you shall love the Lord your God with all your heart, and with all your soul, and with all your might" (Deut. 6:4). This is the love that Paul tells us "bears all things, believes all things, hopes all things, endures all things. Love never ends" (1 Cor. 13:7, 8). This is the love that is necessarily extreme because it is unrestricted, unlimited, unconditional. It is the love that is poured into our hearts by the Holy Spirit who is given to us. It is human because it exists in human hearts; it is divine because God is its source and its object.

This love is the core and essence and center of the Christian life; and when it develops in the human heart it becomes nothing less than

LOVE: HUMAN AND DIVINE

mysticism. At first it may be a tiny spark, scarcely recognizable, quietly drawing one into the cloud of unknowing, into a love for solitude and silence, into a longing for the infinite. But gradually, if one is attentive, it becomes a raging fire that beautifully possesses the whole person. It becomes what the author of *The Cloud* calls "a blind stirring of love," a movement at the ground or core of one's being that is "blind" or "naked" because it is not invested with words and concepts. This love has no human explanation—it is what Ignatius calls "consolation without previous cause." This is the love that inspired St. John of the Cross to sing:

> O Living flame of love
> That tenderly wounds my soul
> In its deepest center![1]

Sometimes this love arises in the heart of a child and is his or her guiding light all through life. At other times it comes later through conversion. It is indeed a sign of the direct action of God in a sinful world.

Now I have said that this love is unlimited, unrestricted, unconditional. I do not mean by this that it is perfect (for perfect love does not exist in weak human hearts) but that it goes on and on and on—and God is its object. But now let me add that this love can be directed not only to God but also to men and women. First, it can be directed towards the Risen Jesus who is at the same time human and divine. How powerfully it is directed towards him in that great scene (the climax of the fourth gospel) where Thomas kneels before him with the words: "My Lord and my God!" (John 20:28). Or again when Peter protests with pain: "Lord, you know everything; you know that I love you" (John 21:17). In both these cases the love that is agape is unlimited, unrestricted, unconditional.

But (and this is important) if this love can be directed towards Jesus it can be directed towards all men and women, who are his members and of whom he has said: " . . .As you did it to one of the least of these my brethren, you did it to me" (Matt. 25:40). What profound agape reigned in the heart of the Good Samaritan! Luke is obviously stressing that the Samaritan's love was unlimited. He simply could not do enough for the unfortunate Jew who had been robbed and beaten and lay by the roadside. He poured oil and wine on his wounds; he put him on his horse; he brought him to the inn; he paid money; he said he would come back to pay more. On and on it goes. Nothing is too much.

III

The deep unconditional love that we call agape may at first be directed toward many people, but it ends up as a single all-embracing love. This is the experience of many people who come to love another or others very, very deeply—and discover that they are possessed by a love that goes far beyond the loved person or persons to the whole human race, to its head, the one man Jesus Christ and to the Father. They express this experience by saying that they see Christ in the face of another or that they experience his presence in the company of another or others.

And is this not closely related to the old philosophical problem of "the one and the many"? Philosophers from the time of Parmenides have known that as the mind penetrates more and more deeply into reality it discovers that while there are many things, there is ultimately only one thing. And so they have asked: "How can there be many things and yet one thing?" And in a parallel way the mystics ask: "How can there be many loves yet only one love?" The theological question is anguishingly complex; the existential answer is disarmingly simple.

This problem is posed in a well-known zen koan:

> A monk asked Joshu, "If all things return to the one, where does the one return to?"
>
> Joshu said: "When I was in the province of Sei I made a robe which weighed seven pounds."[2]

Here we have the contrast between "all things" and "one thing." And the person who would solve this koan must become the one thing that is at the same time many things. For the Buddhist this one thing is the Buddha nature, which is also the true self. This koan, I might add, is surrounded by supplementary sayings such as: "When a single flower blooms, it's spring everywhere," and "One speck of plum blossoms and the three thousand worlds are fragrant." It all recalls the English poet who saw the universe in a grain of sand; it recalls the Christian belief that God, the All, is fully present in every speck of matter in the universe.

The point I wish to make here, however, is that the person who lives the Christian life intensely comes to realize that there are many persons yet there is only one person. There are many loves yet there is only one love. As Mary who sat at the feet of Jesus realized that one thing is necessary, so the Christian realizes that one thing is necessary. Yet the many chores of Martha must also be done.

Let me approach all this from another angle. We know that love tends toward union and that we long to be one with what we love. Human love drives us to be one with the person or persons whom we love: divine love drives us to be one with the All. The poetry of St. John of the Cross vibrates with the poignant cry of one who longs for union, who longs for vision.

And, of course, suffering is built into love, because the union for which love craves cannot be found in this mortal life. We cannot be totally and completely united with another person, and we cannot be totally and completely united with God. Hence the agony of the mystics and their longing for a death that alone is the gateway to final union. Remember how Paul writes to the Philippians: "My desire is to depart and be with Christ, for that is far better" (Phil. 1:23). And St. John of the Cross begs God to tear away the veil of mortal life that separates him from the Beloved: "Tear through the veil of this sweet encounter."[3] Here is the suffering of one who *loves* God passionately but cannot *know* him adequately. Put in scholastic terms, it is the suffering of one who possesses God in the will but whose intellect, darkened by faith, is deprived of vision.

And here, strangely enough, is a vital and practical meeting point between Christianity and Buddhism. For although Buddhism says nothing about a wound of love, it is totally centered on union, on oneness, on non-dualism, and it claims that my greatest sin is my separated self. Moreover, in Buddhist meditation all the emphasis is placed precisely here. But the West, alas, has been too, too quick to label the Buddhist experience "monistic" whereas in fact (and here the dialogue becomes very relevant) this so-called monism can remind us of a powerful Christian truth that has too often been obscured. I mean the truth of the unity of all things and our oneness with God. Yes, we have always known this intellectually; but often, too often, we have failed to recognize the practical consequences for the Christian life. If we really lived the gospel, particularly the fourth gospel, we might find ourselves surprisingly united with Buddhists. Here again inculturation in oriental Buddhist cultures will help Christianity to understand itself richly.

IV

But now let me say a word about the characteristics of friendship, remembering that this is a relationship that may come to exist between man and wife, between parents and children, between teacher and disciple, between celibate persons or between any combination of these.

The first characteristic of friendship is that it is mutual. In this it differs from the love of the good Samaritan or anyone who loves his or her enemies. Just as God wishes us to return his love ("We love because he first loved us" [John 4:19]), and just as the love of God is somehow incomplete unless a return is made, so human love is incomplete when the reciprocal dimension is absent. But when love is reciprocated in such a way that two people love one another deeply at the core of their being, mysticism can reach its peak in a felt presence of the Risen Jesus.

But to reach this point the people involved must not only love; they must also accept love. Just as Jesus stands at the door and knocks, waiting for the other to open and invite him to the inner banquet, so human beings may have to wait at the door. Nor is it easy to open the door to another person. There is a human tendency to resist the invasion from the lover who stands outside, knocking. There is a human tendency to keep the door shut and allow no one, not even God, to enter. So often we are fearful, threatened by the loving intruder. And yet as long as we keep that door closed we can never be intimate with another.

But if we open the door and allow the loved one to enter, we are changed—changed in our very identity. We are emptied of ourselves to be filled with the other. And this can at first be an intoxicating and disturbing experience. But in the end we are emptied of self to be filled not only with the other but also with God.

And by opening the door we make a commitment; and this is a second characteristic of friendship. The love we receive from the other cannot remain dormant within us. It ricochets back on the other and something new is formed through the love of two people. Now there begins a love affair that may be full of struggle and anguish and insecurity—a love affair in which fidelity is the key. This is particularly true in marriage, where vows are made until death. Here fidelity is only possible through agape which is unlimited and unrestricted and which never ends; agape is a manifestation of the divine in the human.

Yet another characteristic of friendship is self-revelation. This point is made by Jesus when he says that the servant does not know what his master is doing but "I have called you friends, for all that I have heard from my Father I have made known to you" (John 15:15). This self-revelation takes place slowly and quietly between two people who are attentive to one another, understand one another, know one another, love one another. In this way I become the mirror in which the other sees himself or herself; and the other becomes the mirror in which I see myself. Yet this takes time. For much dust, much dust, must be removed from that mirror.

At the Johannine Last Supper the disciples were at last beginning to see into the transparent mirror that was Jesus, and there they saw the Father. "He who has seen me has seen the Father . . ." (John 14:9). And there may come a time when friends can borrow the very words of Jesus. They have become other Christs in whom the image of the Father is reflected.

The Way of Friendship

I

It is clear, then, that friendship is a profoundly Christian value. Jesus himself is the great friend. He was a friend not only to the twelve apostles but also to Lazarus and Martha and Mary. So great was his love that he laid down his life for his friends. So great was his intimacy that he told them to dwell in him as he in them; and he led them to dwell with him in the Father. Moreover the friendships of Jesus did not end with his earthly life. Risen and in glory he is the supreme friend to millions of Christians who receive him in the

Eucharist and who confide in him in times of sorrow and in times of joy—and who go with him to the Father. Realization of this has inspired holy men like Thomas à Kempis to write with tender devotion about familiar friendship with Jesus: "Love him and keep him for your friend who when all others leave you will not abandon you nor suffer you to perish in the end."[4] In these words à Kempis stresses the fidelity of Jesus. "Having loved his own who were in the world, he loved them to the end" (John 13:1).

And Jesus told his disciples to love one another as he had loved them, thus making friendship a central value in the Christian life. And it has been so since the earliest times, shining out with special splendor in the writings of Bernard of Clairvaux, Aelred of Rievaulx and other monks of the Cistercian tradition. Appealing to the scriptures as well as to Aristotle and Cicero, the great Cistercians initiated a theology of friendship—which, alas, was never adequately developed. But even if the theology was weak, friendship was always a central value in the Christian life. I recall the deep love which existed between Ignatius and Xavier—and how Xavier read his friend's letters on his knees, often with tears. And then there are classical friendships like that between Francis de Sales and Jeanne Frances de Chantal.

In the Christian life, however, friendship is not only a source of great joy, it is also a way to enlightenment and to union. And in what follows I would like to discuss this aspect of friendship.

II

I have already said that love, human and divine, longs for union— union with other persons and union with the All. Now in human beings union can be enacted at various levels, of which the most obvious in the man-woman relationship is the physical, sexual level. Clearly this is of great significance, and upon it depends the survival of the human race. But in a love relationship it is by no means the central thing. Indeed, it is a truism to say that men and women can be united physically while remaining strangers in mind and heart, and they can be spiritually united without the physical expression that is sexual union. This has led some psychologists to see a spiritual dimension to sexuality. They will say that a man is most man not in his body but in his mind and heart, as a woman is most a woman not in her body but in her psyche and soul. And the man-woman union that takes place at the spiritual and psychological level is powerfully creative. Indeed, physical union, ideally speaking, is a bodily expression of this deep love—a bodily expression that does not create love even though, in married life, it fosters and heals and strengthens the love that is already present and longs to grow.

The great challenge, then, is a union of mind and heart through which people of the same sex or of the opposite sex, entering into deep friendship may reach enlightenment, find their true selves, transcend themselves and together cry out: "Abba, Father!" A challenge indeed this is.

For just as St. John of the Cross suffered in his longing for union with the All, so men and women suffer in their longing for union with one another. They suffer because there are all kinds of barriers keeping them apart—barriers that are mostly invisible because they live in the unconscious mind. I speak of fear, anxiety, guilt, anger, hatred and all kinds of blockages of which people are scarcely aware. Here again we are up against the awful havoc that has been wrought in the personal and collective unconscious by what Christians call original sin. Buddhists recognize something similar (their meditation makes them recognize it) and, like Christians, they maintain that the most terrible wound is isolation, separation, the inability to communicate, the loss of oneness. In its extreme form this is hell, and, alas, there is a trace of hell in every man and woman.

For Jung this chaos is partly caused by damaged archetypes— figures split off from the personality and living autonomously in the unconscious. Of these the most important for our present consideration are the *anima* in the man and the *animus* in the woman; and about these a word may not be out of place.

We now know that no human being is completely masculine or completely feminine. Just as the complementary *yin* and *yang* run all through nature, so there is a feminine dimension in man corresponding to the *yin* and a masculine dimension in woman corresponding to the *yang*. And just as Chinese medicine aims at balancing the *yin* and *yang* in the human body, so Jungian psychology aims at balancing the masculine and feminine, known as the *animus* and the *anima*, in the human psyche. Let me here quote a few lines from Jung:

Every man carries within him the eternal image of a woman, not the image of this or that particular woman, but a definite feminine image. This image is fundamentally unconscious, an hereditary factor of primordial origin engraved in the living organic system of the man, an imprint or "archetype" of all the ancestral experiences of the female, a deposit, as it were, of all the impressions ever made by woman—in short, an inherited system of psychic adaptation. Even if no women existed, it would still be possible, at any given time, to deduce from this unconscious image exactly how a woman would have to be constituted psychically. The same is true of woman: she too has her inborn image of man. Actually, we know from experience that it would be more accurate to describe it as an image of *men*, whereas in the case of the man it is rather the image of *woman*. Since this image is unconscious, it is always unconsciously projected upon the person of the beloved, and is one of the chief reasons for passionate attraction or aversion.[5]

The man who has not integrated his *anima* projects it upon a woman, and likewise the unintegrated woman projects her *animus* upon the man. And while this projection continues, they may be wildly in love, but neither is inwardly free. For they are, to a certain extent, loving and hating themselves in the other, so that they become possessive, or jealous, or manipulative or eager for conquest. The fact is that through these unconscious figures men and women are often bogged down in an infantile relationship with father or mother that needs to be purified and healed.

While the *animus* and *anima* live in the unconscious they are troublesome and can even lead men and women to destruction; but once integrated they give wholeness and beauty and strength to the man or woman who possesses them. Jung loved his own *anima*, as is obvious from his autobiography. He revels in dialogue with this woman within. He finds her a source of inspiration and profound wisdom.

At this point let me digress for a moment to observe that, in my opinion, most of the masculine mystics had a very powerful *anima*, which they succeeded in accepting and integrating through much struggle. A typical example is St. John of the Cross who, in his poetry, identifies with the love-sick bride. A couple of decades ago this puzzled and embarrassed many pious Christians—a celibate man who speaks of himself as the bride! But in the light of Jungian insights it is all very normal; for a man can identify with his femininity and a woman with her masculinity. Indeed, only the well integrated man or woman can do this; and the fact that a certain culture is perplexed by the language of St. John of the Cross or Bernard of Clairvaux shows that this culture has sadly rejected its contrasexual dimension. But let me return to the integration of the *anima* and the *animus*.

A Jungian scholar, claiming that this integration ordinarily comes during, or after, mid-life, describes the interior harmony that it brings. Jolande Jacobi writes:

> Once we have perceived the contrasexual element in ourselves and raised it to consciousness, we have ourselves, our emotions, and affects reasonably well in hand. Above all we have achieved a real independence and with it, to be sure, a certain isolation. In a sense we are alone, for our "inward freedom" means that a love relation can no longer fetter us; the other sex has lost its magic power over us, for we have come to know its essential traits in the depths of our own psyche. We shall not easily "*fall*" in love," for we can no longer lose ourselves in someone else, but we shall be capable of a deeper love, a conscious devotion to the other. For our aloneness does not alienate us from the world, but only places us at a proper distance from it. By anchoring us more firmly in our own nature, it even enables us to give ourselves more unreservedly to another human being, because our individuality is no longer endangered.[6]

This integration is nothing other than an interior marriage, a *conjunctio oppositorum*, a union of the masculine and the feminine in the human person. It makes possible union with other persons, a union in which there is little projection and in which inordinate clinging and anxiety are greatly reduced. Now it becomes possible to love and appreciate and relish the other as other without dragging him or her to myself. Now I can become the clear mirror in which the other sees himself or herself; now he or she can become the clear mirror in which I see myself. Now I have an openness that allows the other to enter and celebrate the loving banquet.

But how does this limpid openness come about? And how do the barriers fall down?

Jung has outlined his own spiritual path with its analysis of dreams and its healing of the psyche. But I believe that a similar end has been attained through prayer, the Eucharist, devotion to the Virgin Mary and other practices of the Christian life. But above all it has been attained through persevering charity—love for one's neighbor and for the poor, as well as through fidelity in the friendship I have been speaking about. By fidelity I mean the will to continue in spite of failures, disappointments, frustrations, set-backs. The person who is able to "bear all things, hope all things, endure all things . . ." will come through. But this is only possible with the help of Another.

III

But such beautiful friendship is not the end; for human nature has been called to divinization, and God became man in order that man might become God. But here it is necessary to recall that there are ordinary and extraordinary friendships. In this respect friendship is like prayer.

The old authors used to speak about ordinary prayer which was available to all Christians and of an extraordinary prayer which was a charismatic gift. In a certain sense this extraordinary prayer was very ordinary, very simple, very unspectacular; but it was also very powerful and no one could force it to happen. One had to wait for the gift.

And in the same way I believe that in the Christian life there are ordinary and extraordinary friendships. In these latter, extraordinary powers of loving are awakened in the human heart and one is truly in love not only with another person but with humanity and with God. Yet the experience of this friendship (like the experience of the most sublime prayer) is also very ordinary, very simple, very unspectacular; for it is a shared mysticism, a shared infused contemplation. No one can force such friendship to arise; it is a gift and a grace. It is a manifestation of the divine in the human, a manifestation of the presence of God in sinful men and women.

For such friendship is modeled on the relationship of Jesus to the men and women whom he loved. Remember how he told his disciples to dwell in him as the branches dwell in the vine: "Abide in me, and I in you" (John 15:4). And by dwelling in him they would dwell in the Father as the Father dwelt in them. Indeed he prayed that human friendship would be a reflection of his love for the Father— "that they be one, Father, as I in thee and thou in me, that they may be one in us . . ." (John 17:21). But he also asked for heroic unselfishness when he said: "If you loved me, you would have rejoiced, because I go to the Father . . ." (John 14:28). Jesus here speaks of a joy that may be filled with emptiness and pain. The joy and the suffering of separation!

These passages of the fourth gospel are pointing toward an experience of indwelling that will only be complete in the resurrection at the parousia. But in this mortal life a foretaste of such union is possible, and it is found when two people meet at the core of their being and the center of the soul. They may be of the same sex or of the opposite sex, for their union goes far beyond such differences to the heart of the divine. This meeting is a profound enlightenment that shakes the universe. In this shared intimacy and mutual indwelling there is a oneness with Jesus whereby the friends cry out in unison: "Abba, Father!"

But now it becomes necessary to say a word about celibacy.

IV

From the dawn of Christianity celibacy or virginity in imitation of Jesus and the Virgin Mary was held in high esteem. In the early church it was associated with martyrdom, not because martyrdom was painful but because it was an expression of, and witness to, the highest love: "Greater love has no man than this, that a man lay down his life for his friends . . ." (John 15:13). And so, in a way similar to martyrdom, celibacy was considered as an expression of, and witness to, the highest Christian love which is agape.

Furthermore, the early church distinguished between celibacy as a charism and celibacy as an ascetical achievement. This latter, the violent conquest of sexual passion, highly esteemed in some religions, was never considered a Christian virtue. Celibacy was rather explained by the fact that some people are drawn beyond sexual passion to a love that is unlimited, unrestricted and unconditional. This love in its intense form is nothing other than mysticism. It is the blind stirring of love, the living flame of love; and it inexplicably draws some people to choose celibacy "for the kingdom." "Not all men can receive this precept, but only those to whom it is given" (Matt. 19:11). Consequently celibate love has always been a pearl of great price in the Christian treasury.

When I speak of celibate love, however, it should be noted that this is not the prerogative of consecrated celibates. Married people are also called to practice profound celibate love. When married persons devote themselves to the service of the poor and afflicted and the oppressed, they practice celibate love. When they love friends and relatives other than their marriage partner, they practice celibate love. When they love one another and refrain for a time from sexual relations—and, as we know, married people sometimes feel called to practice such continence—their love is celibate. And often they experience, no less than consecrated celibate people, the power of such celibate love. My point, then, is that celibate love is an integral and powerful part of the Christian life, whether that life be lived in marriage or in virginity.

Now it often happens that consecrated celibates of the same sex or of the opposite sexes become intimate friends. Such a friendship may arise after mid-life when two people already mature have reached a deep stage of psychological integration through prayer and solitude and silence. Now they come to love one another deeply and radically with a love that goes far beyond the sexual and erotic expression that is part of married life. Since their contrasexual dimension is more or less integrated, they are greatly freed from need and clinging and hunger. Nevertheless, the desire for physical sexual expression may arise; but they can easily transcend this because they are conscious of a unitive and mystical love that transcends physical sexuality and is filled with the presence of God. This is a love that can be compared to the love of Jesus for Mary Magdalen and her love for him. And Christian history abounds in examples of such extraordinary friendship between mystics.

At other times celibate people at a less advanced stage of contemplation are drawn into deep friendship. Since they are still immature and since their *animus* or *anima* is not yet integrated, they must struggle for liberation from possessiveness and selfishness so as to love maturely. And they grow by fixing their eyes on the ideal of loving friendship that fills the pages of the fourth gospel. Guided by this love they forego the sexual intimacy that is part of married life and cultivate the chastity demanded by their vows of celibacy. This is not easy. For they feel the lure of Eve—they may even feel it violently—but they are determined to transcend it so as to enter into that celibate relationship that is a mirror of the life of the triune God. And as they walk this path they are liberated and healed, and they find that their hearts are opening not only to one another but to all men and women and to the presence of Another who is always with them.

And this is possible because they have experienced, at least in some small way, that mystical love which issues from the center of the soul and from those deep caverns in which the Spirit dwells. This is the love which dwells in those realms of the soul where one experiences consolation without previous cause—the secret realms far removed from intellect and sense, far removed from sexual passion and erotic desire.

Obviously this is a difficult and challenging path. It is filled with struggle; it demands sacrifice; it calls for heroic faith; it is for people who love solitude and aspire to mysticism. For it is built on that mystical love that grows in silence and "bears all things, believes all things, hopes all things, endures all things" (1 Cor. 13:17). Those who walk this path may sometimes fall by the wayside or collapse in the mud, but this is no tragedy if they get up and continue on their way. The danger, it seems to me, comes not from human weakness but from the wiles of one who disguises himself as an angel of light. Yes, the danger comes from the subtle and crafty serpent who raised his seductive head in Paradise: "You will be like God. . . . Then the eyes of both were opened, and they knew that they were naked. . ." (Gen. 3:5–7). The human capacity for self-deception is just incredible. Our strength is in humility. Our trust is in the tender love and protection of another woman who crushed the head of the serpent that lay in wait for her heel.

V

I have spoken about celibacy and celibate love, but it is easy to see how a similar journey is possible within marriage. For Christian marriage is based upon that unrestricted agape which Paul highlights when he writes to the Ephesians: "Husbands, love your wives, as Christ loved the church" (Eph. 5:25). And Paul asks husbands to lay down ther lives for their wives as Christ laid down his life for the church. He tells them to love their wives as they would love themselves and their own bodies. This is indeed a remarkable union.

And it is attained through the same struggle, through the same falling of barriers, through the same integration of the personality.

Needless to say, in marriage the erotic and sexual dimension is splendidly lived out in a total self-giving and the mutual love ordinarily extends to children and to children's children. But the ideal, which usually comes late in life, is the shared intimacy, the total indwelling, the union at the center of the soul, the image of the triune God.

Yet in both marriage and celibacy, however great the love, the intimacy, the sharing, one comes to realize that the important thing in this relationship is the presence of the Other. One comes to realize, perhaps sadly at first, that man and woman are not made for one another but for God. One comes to realize that men and women are fellow travelers on the road to Emmaus. They help one another, share with one another, encourage one another, love one another. But the human heart was made for the infinite; and the ultimate love affair is not between man and woman, or between woman and man, but between the human person and God.

Love and Death

I

Jesus lays down his life for his friends as the Good Shepherd lays down his life for his sheep. He loves his friends and he is glad to die for them. His life is not taken away from him: "No one takes it from me, but I lay it down of my own accord" (John 10:18).

And it was total death. "Eli, Eli, lama sabach-thani?" (Matt. 27:46). The Father seemed far away. And of his very friends and of the whole human race it had been said: "They shall look on him whom they have pierced" (John 19:37).

And in those sad days when he was crucified and his body lay in the tomb, the disciples died also. They did not die physically; but there was a very real psychological and emotional death. Peter died; John died; Thomas died. The mother of Jesus died as she stood at the foot of the cross. They all died. And the two disciples who walked to Emmaus expressed the feelings of the group: "But we had hoped . . ." (Luke 24:21).

But through this shattering death a new relationship was born. For there is a mysterious connection between death and birth, between the suffering of the mother and the birth of her child: "When a woman is in travail she has sorrow . . . but I will see you again and your hearts will rejoice, and no one will take your joy from you" (John 16:21, 22). Yes, the disciples discovered that through their suffering and through the death of Jesus something new was born: a new relationship was born, a relationship of total indwelling. The barriers of separation and isolation had fallen down, giving place to a wonderful union, a mutual interiority and an extraordinary shared intimacy. Now the Risen Jesus was dwelling in them. Now they could utter the words which Paul was to cry: "I live, now not I, but Christ lives in me" (Gal. 2:20). Now it made sense to dwell in Jesus as the branches in the vine. Now it made sense to dwell in Jesus as he dwelt in them and as all dwelt in the Father. Now they could understand those mysterious words that later appear in the fourth gospel: "He who eats my flesh and drinks my blood abides in me, and I in him" (John 6:56).

Such a relationship was quite impossible before the death of Jesus and the seeming "death" of those he loved. While Jesus remained on earth his union with them was necessarily limited and imperfect. He had to suffer. He had to die. And he said so, quite clearly: "Nevertheless I tell you the truth: it is to your advantage that I go away . . ." (John 16:7). As if to say that he had to separate himself from his disciples. "For if I do not go away, the Counselor will not come to you . . ." (John 16:7). It is as though Jesus were saying: "I must go away so that I can come again in another form, and there will be a renewed intimacy between us, in such wise that I will dwell in you and you in me." This is the union that reaches its peak when he breathes on them: "Receive the Holy Spirit . . ." (John 20:22). Now the Spirit of Jesus enters into them and they are other Christs, one with him and one with the Father. No longer can there be any separation. Jesus will be with them to the close of the age. That is why they return to Jerusalem with great joy.

II

And is not this pattern repeated in all love relationships? Is not death inevitable in marriage, in friendship, in filial piety, in parental care, in commitment to a community, in a vow to God? "By this we know love, that he laid down his life for us; and we ought to lay down our lives for the brethren" (1 John 3:16).

There are many kinds of death. There is the torture of physical death which the martyrs gladly accepted. There is the psychological and emotional death that comes from separation, from loss, from seeming rejection, from disappointment, from failure. There is the death that necessarily comes to one who passes through the darkness, leaving what is familiar to enter unknown territory and unfamiliar realms of experience. There is a death like that of Paul who could exclaim: "For his sake I have suffered the loss of all things . . ." (Phil. 3:8). Union with the one he loved was bought at a high price. He had to die.

Of course, no one wants to die; and the big temptation is to give up, to throw in the towel, to turn back. Or the temptation is to turn aside to other, superficial relationships that are sensible, attractive, intoxicating, much more fascinating than the obscurity of the dark night.

In all this, Christians can derive inspiration and strength from the example of Buddhist resolution. The words "Even if I die . . ." are ever on the lips of the Bodhisattva. "Even if I die I will go through." And the halls of the Buddhist temple resound with the inexorable chant of those earthshaking vows:

> Sentient beings are innumerable
> I vow to enlighten them
> The passions are inexhaustible
> I vow to extinguish them
> The dharma teachings are immeasurable
> I vow to master them
> The Buddha way is endless
> I vow to follow it

Nor is this an empty formula. For the committed Buddhist to turn back is the supreme betrayal. How well he can identify with those words of Jesus: "No one who puts his hand to the plow and looks back is fit for the kingdom of God" (Luke 9:62). And so he says: "Even if I die . . ."

John Henry Newman, in a famous phrase, said that a thousand difficulties do not make a doubt. He meant that one can and must face all the difficulties, all the fears, all the anguish. One can and must face the possibility of losing one's sanity and losing one's life. But this need not shake one's resolution and one's faith. "Even if I die . . ."

For what sustains a relationship and makes it permanent and immortal is the unrestricted and unconditional love that is at once human and divine. It is human because it is the deepest reality in the human heart: it is divine because it is a gift from on high and is the very presence of God in man. Nor is this love blind. It gives light and shows the way. The knowledge that comes from this religious love I call faith.

And it is precisely here that Christians and Buddhists find union. It is precisely here that we can join hands and march forward. Both religions speak about faith—about that faith which is total commitment and which endures all things. It is true that the object of our faith is not the same; it is true that our devotions differ. But we strive to be unconditionally committed to truth; and our inner disposition, our inner dynamism, our inner resolution are very similar. Together we can cry: "Even if I die . . ."

NOTES

1. *The Living Flame of Love*, St. 1.
2. *Hekiganroku*, Case 45.
3. *The Living Flame of Love*, St. 1.
4. *De Imitatione Christi*, Bk. II, c.7.
5. *Collected Works*, Vol. 17, p. 198.
6. Jolande Jacobi, *The Psychology of C. G. Jung* (New Haven, Conn.: Yale University Press, 1964), p. 119.

Epilogue

T HROUGHOUT EAST ASIA one can see exquisite statues of
 Kannon or Kuan-yin, the Bodhisattva of boundless compassion
who vowed to save all sentient beings. Originally a man, attendant
of the Buddha Amida, Kannon was later represented with female
features and came to be known as a woman. In time of persecution
the Japanese Christians made statues of Kannon to venerate Mary,
the Mother of Jesus. Many of these statues still survive as treasures
of art and religion. And the lady they represent is called "Maria
Kannon."

The word Kannon, originally Kan-ze-on, means "the one who
listens to the sounds of the world." And it was said that Kannon got
enlightenment by listening to every sound. Just by listening to the
sound of the rain and the wind and the river and the waterfall. Just
listening! And through this acute and intense awareness she came to
the great enlightenment that made her one with the universe.

Kannon, then, means "the one who listens to every sound." But
there is another translation which is more in keeping with Kannon's
immense compassion and love. According to this, Kan-ze-on means:

The one who listens
To the cries of the poor

or

The one who listens
To the suffering of the world

And here, I believe, we discover the authentic Kannon who has caught the imagination of millions of Asian people who look to her with hope and trust.

For here we have a Kannon who listens with compassion to the desperate cries of the poor, the sick, the lame, the blind, the afflicted, the disabled, the downtrodden, the naked and the dying. Anyone who suffers can be sure of compassionate understanding from her who listens to the cries of the poor.

And, it is interesting to note, her features are not contorted with anguish and pain. On the contrary, a gentle smile of compassion plays almost imperceptibly around those delicate lips, and her whole body radiates peace. So great is her love that she has refused to enter *nirvana* until all sentient beings are saved. And there she stands, on the pedestals of Asia, exquisitely carved in wood, in bronze and in stone, listening, listening to the cries of the poor.

II

And we can all learn much from Kannon. We, too, can listen to every sound. As we walk through the forest we can be aware of the rustle of the leaves, of the wind in the trees, of all the sounds in that magic world. Or as we walk beside the ocean we can listen to the roar of the waves, the cry of the gulls, the crunch of our feet on the sand. Even in the big city we can listen to the roar of engines, the tooting of horns, the blast of sirens. And as we listen attentively to all those sounds that most people strive desperately to shut out, we come to revel in those much neglected senses, and we discover that at the heart of every sound reigns a mystical silence. And we are not far from enlightenment.

But from Kannon we can also learn to listen to the cries of the poor, cries which in our day rise up with a desperation unknown in the

173

history of the world. From Kannon we can learn to listen to the cries of the oppressed, the exploited, the enslaved, the tortured, the rejected, the hunted, the underprivileged, the handicapped, the victims of injustice, the victims of violence. All these cries are a very real part of our world and we must not, we cannot, stop our ears.

But when we listen, listen, listen to all these cries we come up against something more terrible than suffering. We come up against evil: against naked hatred and injustice and ruthlessness and exploitation. And what a shock this is!

But the most terrible shock is yet to come.

While I read about the big, bad world in the newspaper over my morning coffee, I am comfortably aware that all the evil is "out there," far from me, something to be attacked by my self-righteous ego. Terrible indeed, but far removed. But when I listen, listen, listen like Kannon, I discover that the evil is not only "out there"; it is also in me. I am part of it. And this can be a shattering discovery. Yes, as I listen, listen, listen, I discover within myself the violence and hatred and anger that is shaking the world outside. It is inside and outside, within and around. I see my own appalling capacity for evil. I am a mirror that reflects the suffering and evil of the world.

This can be an almost intolerable experience. The bravest man or woman wants to run away, to escape. Anything but this vision of horror and of hell! And it is then that one must remember Kannon who preferred to stay, who refused to enter *nirvana* until all sentient beings were saved. She listened, listened, listened to the cries of the poor; she shared their suffering; she identified with them; and she came to a wonderful enlightenment from which issued the compassion that has brought comfort and solace to millions of Asians. I, too, if I persevere and pass through the angry darkness will discover in myself not only the evil and suffering of the world—at a deeper level I will discover the grandeur and beauty of God. And from this deep center will flow the gentle compassion that will heal my wounded self and the wounded world.

III

In all this I am thinking, of course, of the immense social problems that afflict us today and their relationship to the prayer and meditation about which I have written in this book. We cannot hope for any solution to these problems unless, like Kannon, we listen, listen, listen to the cries of the oppressed. Only by listening can we reach the roots; only by listening can we see the real evil that is in ourselves and in the world around; only by listening can we tap the sources of that compassion that alone will heal.

Some people refuse to listen. They prefer to be deaf or blind. And so they manufacture lethal weapons; they drop bombs on innocent people; they pollute the environment of impoverished nations; they exploit and underpay helpless workers in the Third World; they cooperate with all kinds of injustice. But they feel happier when they do not see, or hear about, the consequences of their actions.

Other people listen to some extent. They are acutely aware of the starvation and oppression in various parts of the world and they sincerely want to help. They are good, pious people, often professionally religious people, who kneel on their prie-dieu or sit on their cushion saying: "Lord, Lord!" But nearer home they trample on human rights and crush defenseless people without a qualm. This is because their life is compartmentalized. They hear the cries of some poor people but they are carefully insulated against the cries of those whom they themselves crush—such cries simply do not penetrate to their consciousness. They listen, but not enough.

Other people listen with good will. But the sight of suffering and injustice makes them uncontrollably angry. They find themselves consumed with hatred, and they turn to violence. But violence, as we know, begets violence; and such people frequently destroy themselves and others. If only, like Kannon, they could go through the anger and violence to those inner realms where peace and compassion hold sway! Then they would find that their blinding anger has been transformed into a passionate love for justice and truth.

Other people are more like Kannon. They are completely open. They listen to others and they listen to themselves. Their lives are not compartmentalized. They shut out nothing. If they are Christians, they know that listening to the poor is listening to Jesus himself. Of course they experience, sometimes agonizingly, all the hatred and anger and violence and fear that are part of this attentiveness; but they are not swept away by it. Such people are enlightened and compassionate. They are the salt of the earth.

For the Holy Spirit, the Spirit of Jesus, speaks to such people and guides them, telling them what to do. He may guide some of them in such wise that they only listen—like Kannon their vocation is just to listen until all men and women are saved. He may guide others to pick up the dying in the streets of the big cities and to comfort the sick. He may guide others to fight with their lives for the protection of human rights. He may guide others to oppose the evil structures of a society that enslaves millions of people. But in whatever they do they will have compassion in their hearts and they will love justice. They will have compassion not only for the oppressed but also for the oppressor; they will love justice not only in far-flung lands but in their own garden at home.

And here again is a point where Buddhists and Christians can meet. We can listen to the cries of the poor. And having listened we can join hands in searching for a concrete solution to the many problems that afflict our world.

Index

Body of Christ, as transformation of human body, 65–70
Books, holy. *See* Holy books
Breathing, correct: benefits of, 52; as exercise of faith, 53–54; principles of, 50–51
Breathing that is not breathing, 55–58

Celibacy: of mystics, explained, 124–125, 130; practice of, 165–167
Center that is not a center, 62
Chantal, Jeanne Frances de, 154, 160
Chardin, Teilhard de, 7, 21, 69
Christian tradition of self-realization, 41–47
Clement, 69
The Cloud, 62, 63, 67, 78, 125, 128, 129, 155
Collective self-realization, 32–33
Commentators, biblical, need for and qualities of, 108–110
Commitment, as characteristic of friendship, 158–159
Conscience, supremacy of, 8–9
"Consolation without previous cause," 115, 155
Contemplation, as Jungian way of healing, 147–149
Courtly love, 122–124
Creative, biblical interpreter as, 103–104
Crede ut intelligas, ix, 12, 96
Culture, European, effect on missionaries, 3, 6
Cyclic process, meditation as, 78–79, 84–85

The Dark Night, 118
Dark night: in healing of memory, 134–135; as part of way of affectivity, 116–119
David, identifying with, 101
Death: as life cycle crisis, 141, 144–145; in true love 168–171
Declaration on Religious Freedom, 8
Deeper words, 80–85: exterior words, 83; formal words, 80, 81–82; interior words, 83–84; substantial words, 80, 82; successive words, 80–81; WORD INCARNATE, 84
Devotion, way of, 125–130

Diagram of the Supreme Ultimate, 79
Dialogue between religions: history of, 2–4, 5–7; necessity for, 1–2; precepts for practicing, 10–15; problems with, 15–23
Dodd, C. H., 46
"Dogmatic Reflections on the Knowledge and Self-Consciousness of Christ," 45
Dokusan, 98
"Dungeon Letter," 92

Eating the holy books, 95–96
Eckhart, Meister, 67, 109, 128
The Ecumenist, 18
Eliade, Mircea, 54, 133
Eliot, T. S., 102
Enantiodromia, principle of, 79
Eros and agape, 120–125
Eucharist, as symbol of transformation of human body, 66–70
Eve love, 120–121, 124–125
Examen, 140
Experiencing, as different from knowing, 29, 45
Exterior words, 83

Faith: need for in self-realization, 32; as part of way of breath, 53–54
Feeling, transformation of, 111–130: eros and agape, 120–125; way of affectivity, 112–119; way of devotion, 125–130
First night of mystics, 138–139
Formal words, 80, 81–82
Foucauld, Charles de, 11
Francis of Assisi, St., 122, 123, 124
Freud, Sigmund, 27, 111, 112, 121
Friendship: characteristics of, 158–159; way of, 159–168

Gandhi, Mahatma, 88
Glossolalia, 75
Good, in other religions, recognizing, 8–9
Grace, need for in self-realization, 32
Gregory of Nyssa, 42, 69
Griffiths, Bede, 63